DIANE WAKOSKI

The Archaeology of Movies and Books

VOLUME I: Medea the Sorceress
VOLUME II: Jason the Sailor
VOLUME III: The Emerald City of Las Vegas

BY DIANE WAKOSKI

Coins & Coffins (1962)
Four Young Lady Poets (1962)
Discrepancies and Apparitions (1966)
The George Washington Poems (1967)
Inside the Blood Factory (1968)
The Magellanic Clouds (1970)
The Motorcycle Betrayal Poems (1971)
Smudging (1972)
Dancing on the Grave of a Son of a Bitch (1973)
Trilogy: Coins & Coffins, Discrepancies and Apparitions,
   The George Washington Poems (1974)
The Wandering Tattler (1974)
Virtuoso Literature for Two and Four Hands (1975)
Waiting for the King of Spain (1976)
The Man Who Shook Hands (1978)
Trophies (1979)
Cap of Darkness (1980)
The Magician's Feastletters (1982)
The Collected Greed, Parts 1–13 (1984)
The Rings of Saturn (1986)
Emerald Ice: Selected Poems 1962–1987 (1988)
Medea the Sorceress (1991)
Jason the Sailor (1993)
The Emerald City of
   Las Vegas (1995)

DIANE WAKOSKI

THE EMERALD CITY

OF

LAS VEGAS

BLACK SPARROW PRESS · SANTA ROSA · 1995

ACKNOWLEDGMENTS

These poems, some in slightly different versions, have appeared in the following publications: *Alpha Beat Soup, The Beloit Poetry Journal, The Cafe Review, Caliban, Caprice, Graffiti Rag, The Green Mountain Review, Literature and Medicine, Many Mountains Moving, The Plum Review, The Princeton Chronicle, Puerto Del Sol, Red Cedar Review, River Styx, White Cat, The Collected Greed, Parts 1–13* (Black Sparrow), *The Ice Queen* (Parallel Editions) and *Poems on the Underground.*

Black Sparrow Press books are printed on acid-free paper.

LIBRARY OF CONGRESS CATALOGING–IN–PUBLICATION DATA

Wakoski, Diane.
    The emerald city of Las Vegas / Diane Wakoski.
       p.   cm. — (The Archaeology of movies and books ; v. 3)
    ISBN 0-87685-971-6 (pbk. : alk. paper). — ISBN 0-87685-972-4 (cloth trade : alk. paper). — ISBN 0-87685-973-2 (signed cloth : alk. paper)
    I. Title. II. Series: Wakoski, Diane. Archaeology of movies and books ; v. 3.
PS3573.A42E39   1995
811'.54—dc20   95-18192
                                                         CIP

This book is dedicated to America's mythic city,
Las Vegas

TABLE OF CONTENTS

EMERALD CITY

Looking for Beethoven in Las Vegas 15
Slot Machines 20
So Cold in Winter 21
George Washington at Sam's Town 23

MAGIC SHOES

In St. Louis 29
Wearing the Silver Shoes 31
Roller Skate Jazz 34
Geoffrey Bends to Tie My Shoe 36
She Bends to Offer Me Running Shoes 38
"What Was It Like?" 40
Jewel Leaves 41
The Moon Slides Her Pointed Slipper into the
    Darkening Sky 43
I Come to the Poetry Reading Wearing My New
    Silver Shoes 45

SHAPE SHIFTING

Deer Gods 51
Butterflies Are Shadow Shapes 53
Frightening Green 55
Size 57
Angel Wire 59
Craig's Hummingbirds 62

MAGIC BOOKS

Kelly as the Mage 73
Light 76
Waiting for Jason 77
Emerald City 78
For Linda's Mother 79
For Catherine Who Says She Is Wuthering Heights . . . 81
Parkin 84
Tea Ceremony 87
Unpermitted Silence 87
Desert Nose 88
Malachite 90

MAGIC FLOWERS

Summer Light 95
Violets 96
Queen Anne's Lace 98
Cardinal at the Feeder 101
Flower Parts 101
Sketching Flowers 101
Night 103
The Rosy Trickster, Old Coyote 104
Lily Hands 107

WITCHES

Aging 111
Alexander 111
Our Lady of the Chanterelles 113
Flower Masks 115
Masks 116
The Blue Dress / Airmail Letter 117
Hansel and Gretel 119
The New Moon, a Scar 121
Healing Goddesses 123

Botticelli's Edges 125
Your Sister in Jail 127
White Cat 130
Dogs 131
Fame 131
Swan's Neck 132
I Hammer 135
Eye-Voice 136

THE EMERALD BOOK

The Emerald Book 141
Orchids Growing on the Green Felt 142
Ireland 144
Seeing the World Through Hopper's Glasses 150
White Las Vegas 152
Mary's Diner 154
Autumn 156
The Sadness on Robert's Face 157
Examining Money 160
Anna's Hummingbird 166
The Sun Becomes the Moon 167
Champagne Light 167

EMERALD LIGHT

Luxor 173
Craig's California Fire 174
Ice Walking 175
Winter Sunshine 177
Mystère 179
David's Letter 180
Closet Oaks 182
The Motorcyclist in the Woods 183
From Shells to Radishes 185
Sound Track 187
Broken Ice 189

Stories about My Life 190
Watching the Drinkers of Grand Marnier 192
Saluting the Sun 194
The Butcher's Apron 196
Hot Flickers / Movie Light 199
Starlight 200
Medea's Children 201

THE EMERALD CITY
OF LAS VEGAS

EMERALD CITY

"... if you did not wear spectacles the brightness and glory of the Emerald City would blind you. Even those who live in the City must wear spectacles night and day. They are all locked on, for Oz so ordered it when the City was first built, and I have the only key that will unlock them."

—*the Guardian of the Gates talking to Dorothy*

Then the Guardian of the Gates put on his own glasses and told them he was ready to show them to the palace. Taking a big golden key from a peg on the wall he opened another gate, and they all followed him through the portal into the streets of the Emerald City.

Even with eyes protected by the green spectacles Dorothy and her friends were at first dazzled by the brilliancy of the wonderful City. The streets were lined with beautiful houses all built of green marble and studded everywhere with sparkling emeralds. They walked over a pavement of the same green marble, and where the blocks were joined together were rows of emeralds, set closely and glittering in the brightness of the sun. The window panes were of green glass, even the sky above the City had a green tint, and the rays of the sun were green.

Frank Baum, *The Wizard of Oz*

LOOKING FOR BEETHOVEN IN LAS VEGAS

The music in my head again,
not lily pad orchestra
or ebony flute,
the opening of yucca bells,
a creamy swish of lips,
the waver of pink and yellow,
opuntia, cresting flesh,
ocotillo flame, piercing air,
clear sound of the flowers.

My car pointed West,
the trunk full of diamonds,
and Mother rattler coiled there.
We are traveling to Southern California,
to the Pacific,
where surfers
and angel-boy-men worship sun,
there the Osprey Sisters search for their piano,
where the moon bathes,
and the foggy canyons wrap their shot silk
around old bodies.

Still, there is a destination
which must be accomplished first,
a search for Beethoven in the
casinos of Las Vegas. Why
search for him
in this gaudy city
where ham and eggs are served

24 hours a day?
where dawn is dewy
but freshness is only in the mind,
the carpets permeated with smoke,
the upholstery stale with gin and perfume.
But I heard his sounds there once.

Never, in the subways of my city,
New York:

never, in the pounding of the Atlantic on steeply sloping
    beaches
when the sun nudged my tips
and wound round the sprocket of desire;
never, in the adobe missions
and terra-cotta roofs
of empty California life;
never, in the thick wheat-filled, asparagus-tipped, peach-
    laden, corn-spiked

summers or ice-clotted winters
of Michigan;
not even on the cobblestone streets of Hydra, waking, caught
    like a cormorant,

with the ring around my throat, and looking
deep into the squid-clear Mediterranean;
or in the green-grey olive trees on the rocky hills of Mallorca
where a man in pain was moaning in his cold kitchen.

I listened for his music
as I walked through Beethoven's park
in the Grinzingerstrasse,
Vienna spring, where I did hear
La Traviata and fancied as I wandered through the
    Schönbrunn,
hearing Mozart's piano music accompanying my steps,

but I did not hear Beethoven's music
even elusively,
not once,
till I walked into the MGM Grand Hotel
and heard the thunk thunk thunk
of silver dollars
rattling into the slot machine tubs;
there it was,
thunk, thunk, thunk,
Beethoven's Sixth Symphony;
there it was,
a string quartet;
there it was,
the Appassionata Sonata;
Fidelio;
a Bagatelle;
thunk, thunk, thunk, thunk, thunk, symphonies
in George's coin,
the silver dollar from which
he had his Camp Cup made;
thunk, thunk, thunk,
the history of America,
that is,
the U.S.A.
played in a new symphonic thrust
when those silver dollars
clatter out of the machines in Las Vegas,
in the American desert,
the sound beyond The Strum,
the sound created by Beethoven, Americanized and
wandering in the desert,
looking for someone to love.

So, my journey has taken me there,
aching elbows, old acorns of the East
rattling in my empty joints,
making another music,

this one of aging and bone-crack death,
of sleeping alone and
tending the garden,
of looking out through the lacy curtains of one's life,
seeing the desert as the only future,
no strawberries on the lips now,
or moist cantaloupe.

I hold in my hand a cardboard cup
as big as a child's head.
It is filled with silver dollars
I have received in exchange
for paper money. They weigh
down my hand
as the past has never weighed me down.
It is the future
which now is so heavy,
as heavy as a 6,000 B.T.U. air conditioner
or a small refrigerator,
or a 24″ pot with soil, containing a mountain ash tree.
As heavy as a mortgage and a house
your lover
doesn't want to live in.
It is the prospect of sleeping alone
every night, and the books
no one
will ever read.

When I dream of this city,
Las Vegas, I am
bare-armed,
long-haired,
scented with lilies of the valley
wrapped in raw silk,
shod in glass or gold,
looking nothing like
I ever looked in youth or life,

playing Chemin de Fer,
escorted by a man who wins at the dice tables, and I hear
Beethoven's symphonies
because they are big and melodic and my
life is big and melodic.

But when I am in this mythic city,
I am a small plump woman,
swathed in tent-like clothes,
sitting in the Keno parlor, reading
Henry James and playing 90 cent games.
I listen to the
thundering next to me in the bank
of slot machines, the tinkle,
the ringing,
and the thunk, thunk, thunk, thunk, thunk
of silver dollars
clanking into the metal pans.
It is Beethoven's music
but he is not here.

None of the men I love
are ever where
I look for them.
My map,
the Moon's map:
The *Mare* of Isolation,
The *Mare* of Remote Shadows,
The *Mare* of Longing.
No geography which would ever yield
what I have
searched for.

Driving West,
old, enlightened,
I still cannot fold up those
maps of lost goldmines,

abandoned trunks full of diamonds,
of new countries and other planets.
I still listen for Beethoven at the ocean,
and George Washington in the desert.
But my own voice fades
into the landscape,
perhaps is only heard through
the unspoken language of desert flowers.

Industry types like to remind you that gambling has long
been the American way. After all, the first Continental
Congress helped finance the Revolution with lotteries. Ben-
jamin Franklin, George Washington and Thomas Jefferson
each sponsored private lotteries. Our founding fathers were
just number guys in wigs.

Gerri Hirshey, "Gambling Nation"

SLOT MACHINES

They are nice to you
while you are losing. Never
insult you. Always hunger for your
attention. The men I loved who left me were never so
nice, so willing to keep taking my
love.

SO COLD IN WINTER

and so what:
   that you think about
     Las Vegas all the time?
   that you want to be sitting
     at the blackjack table?
       you want to be watching your run
of bad luck?
       "If I didn't have bad luck,
       I wouldn't have any luck at all,"
         says a character in
      an old movie.
It's early march with snow
and the shadow of a blackbird
on the ground. My fear is of death, my fear
is of pain, my
fears wake me up
in the morning and make me moan,
disturbing my husband sleeping next to me
like a big, kind, wonderful source of heat,
a wood stove or a beautiful ceramic-tiled one;
but he doesn't like my moaning and muttering, my restless
   fears.

If I were in a hotel with him in Las Vegas, I would creep
   out of bed,
get in the shower, warm up, dress, and go down
to the blackjack tables,
where there are mostly tired players who have been up all
   night.

21

They are like an old pack of cards, greasy with handling,
but not ready yet, to be exchanged for a fresh one.
That's when I like to play blackjack, sit at the green felt
tables, 6 a.m., feel the cards, slick as wafers in my hands,
always a surprise, my new stack of chips, the day's money
still intact, usually some odd people sitting down
at the table, and I feeling fresh as snow now, forgetting
how I was moaning in bed, fearing age and death,
fearing disease and rejection, fearing ridicule
and ugliness.

I love the
morning light
when I feel as if I could be
anything,
that my body is fresh and men could
really love me. I lie under the flannel and down covers
on this wintry bed, they are meltingly soft and infinitely
squeezable, and I tell myself that
what other people curse and see
as bad luck perhaps is not
so bad seen in the context of
one's own life.

Not what you don't have,
not all the things which have gone wrong or have never
        gone right,
but that you are still alive, "Lucky Life!" as Whitman says,
knowing that actor was right:
    "If I didn't have bad luck,

    I wouldn't have any luck at all."

Although he helped put it together, Einstein was never satisfied with quantum theory. He didn't like intrinsic randomness ("I cannot believe that God plays dice with the universe"), but most of all he disliked the fact that quantum theory (as interpreted by Bohr and Heisenberg) implies that reality is observer-created. "I cannot imagine," Einstein once said, "that a mouse could drastically change the universe by merely looking at it." Einstein accused Bohr and Heisenberg of attempting to restore man (and mouse) to the center of the cosmos from which Copernicus had ousted them nearly five hundred years ago. "The belief in an external world independent of the perceiving subject," Einstein maintained, "is the basis of all natural science."

Nick Herbert, *Quantum Reality: Beyond the New Physics*

GEORGE WASHINGTON AT SAM'S TOWN⋆

Our Uncle Sam is covered with orchids.
He owns casinos in Las Vegas and Laughlin
where we sleep under sand dunes
and drink cactus water
in the mornings. Because I think about
such things, I always imagine that George Washington
        might be
with me when I gamble

⋆ *Sam's Town is the name of a casino in Las Vegas, neither on the Strip nor Downtown, away from all the regular "action," owned by Sam Boyd, and largely frequented by locals and regular visitors to Las Vegas like my husband and me.*

23

at one of Uncle Sam's casinos. I hover
around the nickel progressive Keno Machines
picking numbers the way I chose husbands:
    with care,
    following my sense of symmetry or shape,
    not ever knowing how one combination might win
    or succeed, surprised when it might,
    doggedly continuing on
    with the game when it doesn't.

Sometimes George smiles his tight
smile at me, but most of the time, I think of him
as my Uncle Elmer who used to hold me when I was a
        colicky baby.
He soothed me, rocked me, the way the numbers do now.
I am glad I'm not a kid any more.
Now my adventures can begin.
Childhood is such a literal time, but as you age
the sand dunes give way
to a place that looks
as if it's covered with date palms.
Sometimes we see a pyramid,
other times a procession to Caesar's Palace, but never
a hint that this desert
could not turn into a jungle
or a movie studio, a circus or a
pirate's ship.

I am baffled by the Chamber of Commerce that seems to
        want to
turn Las Vegas into a kiddy town.
Believe me, this place is not
for kids, since children
don't know how to live in
a fantasy world. Kids need food,
water, a sense of home
and expensive shoes; they need attention, love,

and for the world
to revolve around them. Las Vegas
is the Emerald City which Dorothy,
     ten-year-old Dorothy,
wants to leave
because it's not home.
She knows what children know,
that pretending and fantasy are not for her;
she hasn't yet had
a lifetime of pain,
one that offers no alternative
than a mindwalk to imaginary pleasures.
No, Las Vegas,
like the Emerald City,
is for adults; we are the ones
who know how to live on a desert and pretend
it is a palace, the ones
who can go without food for long periods
of time, who can live
in a world constructed entirely from our own
images, fantasize love,
pretend someone is paying attention,
forget about cheap shoes, imagine we are wearing
magic slippers.

When we are at the casino, we believe
we can have everything, or at least will have it very soon.
We enjoy imagining this
as much as actually achieving it.
Winning is not
absolute,
it's the up after a down,
the moment
     when all the bars line up,
     or there are full houses,
     a straight flush,
     or five numbers out of six.

We don't care about politics
or the stupidity of people who run our lives.
We are rearranging that world
every time we pull a handle,
        push a button
        throw dice,
        lay our chips,
        or play a hand.
George Washington is with me at the blackjack table.
I am wearing the silver shoes / I am in the Emerald City,
wearing the glasses that allow me to see
what the childish Einstein could not understand:

the reason God, if he is an adult,
might play dice with the universe.

MAGIC SHOES

"The Silver Shoes," said the Good Witch, "have wonderful powers. And one of the most curious things about them is that they can carry you to any place in the world in three steps, and each step will be made in the wink of an eye. All you have to do is knock the heels together three times and command the shoes to carry you wherever you wish to go."

Frank Baum, *The Wizard of Oz*

Shoe—a device for multiple-deck games.

Len Miller, *The Gambling Times Guide to Casino Games*

IN ST. LOUIS

The beautiful Helen, whose foot was like
a Calla Lily, came out of an egg
which then turned into an apple of gold,
one that Paris caused so many goddesses to quarrel over,
and finally set men against women, when Eve ate it
in her own garden;
and in St. Louis
they had to discontinue
the famous Easter Egg Hunt
which each year featured one of precious metal,
hidden along with the thousands of edible ones.

Parents got involved,
wanting to find the golden egg themselves,
their children hardly even excuses
for the frantic search,
tearing apart the park,
circumventing other children, even,
beating them up trying to prevent them
from finding it.

My mother hid eggs for us
around the house,
    in the tank which hid the hot water heater,
    in the can that held dust cloths, in
    the medicine cabinet, and on top of the mirrored frame
    around the painting of flamingos in our fifties living
       room
and like little swans, we bent our necks this way and that
       looking

into every hidden spot, even found one under the pedals of
the upright piano.

Two sisters, we quarreled and quarreled,
but never over an egg.
Resting separately, in the refrigerator, was my chocolate egg
with fruit and nuts and her cream-filled one.
There was no golden egg
   to tempt us,
no gold rush,
   to remind us of earlier Argonauts,
   or a Golden Fleece,
no image of a woman
   for whom civilization shaped itself
or a father-lover-god who appeared as a swan or
   a shower of gold. Our daddy
      was in the Navy, a sailor, and we were
         plain girls, like our mother,
not the kind who would inspire gods to love us,
not the kind who could ever keep
   a wandering daddy at home,
   no golden eggs,
   no silver spoons/
   certainly, no silver shoes to take us wherever we might
      want to go.

"I cannot understand why you should wish to leave this
beautiful country and go back to the dry, grey place you call
Kansas."

"That is because you have no brains," answered the girl. "No
matter how dreary and grey our homes are, we people of flesh

and blood would rather live there than in any other country,
be it ever so beautiful. There is no place like home."

Dorothy talking to the Scarecrow
Frank Baum, *The Wizard of Oz*

Dear Jonathan,

I can't bear to let Dorothy have the last word on this
one.

Yr. Lady of Silver Lightning Bolts,

DW

WEARING THE SILVER SHOES

I'd like to hear silver dollars clanking out
of slot machines, instead of the tinkling of silver
as our hostess clears the table.
There was just a bit of white
chocolate mousse left
in the goblet which held it. Before she got up,
I watched her playing with her silver spoon,
the silver twinkling
as she undulated her hand, holding
an image of privilege.

Under the table, my white Nikes
were still, but I thought of the lightning bolts
against my foot, and willed the shoes
to be silver shoes, shoes that would take me anywhere,
away from this table of fat people talking
about school board elections and what it means that
Generation X likes Tony Bennett.
In my lap, my hands were still, fat
age-spotted hands.
I'd like to see a stack of black chips
rising in front of me at the card table
or the black and white dice hitting the sides of the craps table
with numbers I've chosen.

I'd like to feel as passionate about
anything as I do about this food, the way
I've come to love it so much—
its savor and fragrance, its preparation, its presentation.
I'd like to understand why I've displaced Romance
from the center of my table
and why the silver spoons are in
other mouths.

"Are you running away from something?"
you asked. Yes,
from tables with no
silver spoons,
from tables where I am only
the servant.
My feet have always been
like quicksilver messengers and I've loved
the itinerant life.
Instead of a silver spoon
I've had a silver tongue
in my mouth.
Perhaps it's reflected in my quicksilver shoes?
Movement was as silvery as words!

Now, this silver tongue
like the rings of Saturn
is stuck in my mouth; I move it and
move it, in and out, trying to touch the lightning bolts of
     mercury
off these silver shoes which have the power
to take me any place I want to go.

Unlike Dorothy,
I don't think that place is called "home."

"The North is my home," said the old lady, "and at its edge
is the same great desert that surrounds this Land of Oz."

"How can I get there?" asked Dorothy.

"You must walk. It is a long journey, through a country that
is sometimes pleasant and sometimes dark and terrible. How-
ever, I will use all the magic arts I know to keep you from
harm."

...

"The road to the City of Emeralds is paved with yellow
brick," said the Witch.

Frank Baum, *The Wizard of Oz*

ROLLER SKATE JAZZ

                      I am on them, old metal roller skates
clamped to my shoes,
      square platforms rolling
         along the asphalt streets
of La Habra, California. No, this is a wide new road
made only for bicyclists and skaters, winding down to
the Pacific ocean, past our big houses in the Palisades/
the sound of the skate wheel is reassuringly metallic, the
      whirring
of drum brushes, an occasional jazz cymbal clang
as we set a skate down
hard.
   I like the way our arms move

when we skate alone, back and forth, the comfort
of movement rather than pain, the arms
like sea anemones swaying above our bodies.
On this Emerald City road, we can skate and skate
with no sidewalk curbs to jump or negotiate, no bumps
or cracks to slick-in the wheels with nicking or thumping
      sounds
and perturbations. This road is better than yellow brick;
this road is as smooth as desert sand looks from a distance.
It is an ocean of smooth pavement, cresting occasionally, as
      we surf
its black shining surface, smooth as pianos, Bill Evans
playing riffs the way our feet move so naturally,
Eddy Gomez on bass the way we occasionally
pick up the heavy skates

34

and set them down
deliberately.

I think this is the way swimmers feel, but we are on land;
        we're not in cars,
separated from

the road and the earth
by a substantial distance. No, we are not much
more than an inch
away from everything which will engulf us someday. We're
        not
birds, we're human, on our old metal roller skates, clamped
to our leather school shoes, and we are
learning how to live
above the earth, not breaking the connection,
while making it smoother
like piano music
        or water
                or our breath
which glides in and out
        easily when we are not
                sick, not ready to die.
Before it's an effort to walk
    or dance, and
            each foot, like a last chord in "Stella By Starlight"
                comes down to the ground
                        silkily.

She took off her old leather shoes and tried on the silver
ones, which fitted her as well as if they had been made for
her. . . .

Within a short time she was walking briskly toward the Emerald City, her silver shoes tinkling merrily on the hard yellow road.

Frank Baum, *The Wizard of Oz*

GEOFFREY BENDS TO TIE MY SHOE

for Geoffrey Bankowski

Voices are sometimes
rich as the oil of a coffee bean, but never
as pungent. Voices recede. They
are memories,
or the past.

Silence is the presence.

I could turn off every sound
I ever heard. I could purge the voice
of The Motorcycle Betrayer, though
to me it has the resonance
of coffee. I could purge
every voice which
ever loved me,
since love
means something different
to everyone who
feels it.

I could never know what made you kneel

to tie my untied shoe. I seem to ignore the act,
but it is the only thing of this evening
that I remember
significantly.
Who are you, who ties
my shoe? Someone who knows that such gestures
extend beyond the intimate? Someone who
thrills me with what Art does, so much more
than anything personal.
I could connect myself
   to Bob Dylan, the singer
     whose voice ruled mine, this way, and
     it is the one way in which I could connect
     the rest:
     the evening,
     a pleasurable blur—
     food, friends, wine glasses,
     the thought of poetry, the past—
How could any of us say anything?
Words are more
than we can ever know,
yet only
distillations
of touch.
Thank you for wordlessly
tying my shoe tonight.
Wherever you go,
this gesture stays with me:
     you knelt and tied my shoe
     while others talked.
This gesture others hardly noticed,
I take with me to bed tonight.

A modern Knight, you tied my shoe
leaving an image of
a glove, a horse, a rose, perhaps the
shadow of a mirror, Beauty

remembered her Beast,
the sword between two chaste sleepers.
The taste of coffee.
   Such unconnected

connections.

SHE BENDS TO OFFER ME RUNNING SHOES

Her hair, brown as coffee, and ending at

   her shoulders, as if the coffee were being poured
   from a glass pot into a basin, a wide stream/no
   edges for liquids,
flies out. She jumps on the sand, she's playing volleyball,
a game I understand
though have no wish
to ever perform. The hair returns
to its perfect shape, it is like
water, the ocean, like Coca Cola,
a drink, like sweet syrups such as molasses
scraped from the bottom of the rum barrel. She bends
now in her job, fitting athletic shoes on the feet
of women like myself, who are not athletes,
who grew up wearing shoes too narrow or short, too
      pointed
or high, who had no eyes for anything like volleyball
or even running.

I wonder how she can be so helpful, so nice
to someone like me who doesn't have to bend over the
      ugly

inferior feet of the world just when she wants to be out
making her body as perfect
as her waterfall hair.
How cynical I have become that I cannot
believe she actually
enjoys helping people and doesn't mind
tending their
imperfect feet. She knows something I do not know,
and this secret might be one she's learned
doing those things I never
did or thought I could:
   running, standing before a net next to the Pacific Ocean,
   pacing palm-lined neighborhood streets. Or is there
another secret? Even as I sit here
wearing my running shoes, called "Athena"
and knowing my name is Diane: should I be catching the
     glimpse of
a simultaneous past holding a young woman
with a silver bow and quiver of arrows?
her silver foot disappearing into a reflection of this girl's
splashing, coffee-cup hair?

Now the Wicked Witch had a great longing to have for her
own the Silver Shoes which the girl always wore.

The Witch was too much afraid of the dark to dare to go in
Dorothy's room at night to take the shoes, and her dread of
water was greater than her fear of the dark.

Frank Baum, *The Wizard of Oz*

"WHAT WAS IT LIKE?"

my colleague asked me, "your life in New York
when you knew her?" But I could only think
of a dull sentence, like a scuffed shoe in a closet,
and I was ashamed of its rundown heels, misshapen toes. I too
was impressed to find my name in the index of the memoir,
        as if I were
a Capezio or a Donna Karan shoe in her trendy life;
but to me the fact that neither the author nor I
had more than a sentence to say
about each other
meant, not that there were untold stories,
but that there were un-lived stories.

I have always known that we had a history
that we should have acted out,
but in fact, I associated with her only briefly
during that one session of our lives.
In my mind
it has something to do
with my invisible tie to Mormons,
as if the Angel Moroni
watches over me, makes connections. I try to figure out what
this has to do with my life, but it may have nothing
to do with my life, except giving me
a clue
to something I don't understand:

that we have untold
stories.

That maybe in a parallel universe
or the next life
those are the stories we will live. Maybe Twyla
and I have a story to enact together.
If I wrote a memoir, I who love beautiful shoes, I
who love dancing but cannot dance, I
who have some odd connection with Mormons,
and imagine all the time that my life is a ballet, I daresay
I'd put her
in the index too.

Quantum Reality #4: The many-worlds interpretation.
(Reality consists of a steadily increasing number of parallel
universes.)

Nick Herbert, *Quantum Reality: Beyond the New Physics*

JEWEL LEAVES

Why would she leave
her shoe on the steps, even
Cinderella running so fast to be inside
before any prince could see her rags would probably not
have lost just that one item.

One shoe to me
means rape or abduction,

means war and guns, fire, someone
running for her life, or being carried senseless
over a rough shoulder.

Would the glass shatter?
Would a girl who had nothing but
a magic shoe, ever leave it behind, no matter
her hurry?

The oak trees still in their rich summer disguise
mask the house and world beyond my backyard.
I know that on the other side
I wouldn't find Wall Street or The Great Wall of China.
I know that on the other side I'll find a parking lot
with a few old cars, a derelict Weber grill
used by the kids who live in the slightly run-down wooden
house,

but imagine if there were a shoe lying there too
beside one of the metal doors?
Instead, I think
there is a green felt table
where blackjack players
sit in a semicircular fan, the leaves
fall off the oaks
onto their tables, like green jewels,
like worn cards, like success or failure,
like cups of coffee turned cold.

Why would she leave
something which meant so much to her
behind? Unless it was not she
who left it? Or unless
her suitor was not the man
she had once thought him to be?
The cards dealt.
The glasses all now empty?

THE MOON SLIDES HER POINTED SLIPPER INTO THE DARKENING SKY

The man smoking Lucky Strikes,
his desert eyes squinting like Clint Eastwood,
into the darkness of a Manhattan apartment, looking
oh looking for his father's big handed approval

and Steelman, smoking Marlboros,
marine-close haircut outlining his skull,
eyes open to every aspect of light, particles, waves,
the Pacific Ocean foaming next to him in my pillow
where we sleep at night

and I the Sorceress with gold pouring
off my gloved hands, moonlight drifting like
fog or smoke out of my mouth, swirling on some screen
which with trusting eyes I gaze at, like a crystal ball.

Gambler, I'm a gambler/ this stack of poker chips
is moonlight, and the poker hand comes,
the cards click click clicking
like the toenails of a friend's bull terrier on marbled floors
of Viennese palaces and cafes—

There is no unfilled space, no vacuum, no unfilled void
in this universe. And even our lives which often
seem so slight, so lean of substance,
their very space itself is alive, radiant,
lighted, filled until everything is light and sometimes
light filled with light.

I am the woman who believes in incantations,
spells, sleight of hand instead of death. You'll find me in
        vast casinos
or libraries, or empty bedrooms
where the ocean soughs and echoes. I say
I am looking for light, but what I want to find is
perhaps quite different. "Fill light,"
he tells me, "changes the meaning of everything."

This is a law of physics:
each time you pull the handle
of a slot machine you are creating a new sequence.
It is always new, a beginning. Perhaps
every act is connected to the future,
but only randomly. What an effort civilization is
to remember so vividly those random perhaps-chains,
perhaps-sequences, those maybe-patterns that we feel
must shape our lives.

The twisted wisteria vine drips
and drips the message Persephone is waiting
to hear. The moon slides her
pointed slipper into the darkening sky,
fills up the expanse, particulate,
splintered with light,

filled with light.

Quantum Reality #6: Neorealism. (The world is made of
ordinary objects.) The bottom line of many quantum experi-
ments consists of a pattern of tiny flashes on a phosphor
screen. Is it so obvious that such a simple phenomenon—the
basis of all TV images—can be explained only by resorting to

some bizarre quantum reality? Watching those little flashes of light appear on the screen one by one, it's easy to imagine that they are actually caused by little objects—by real electrons with positive and momentum attributes all their own. This common-sense notion that the ordinariness of direct experience can be explained by an equally ordinary underlying reality is the basis for a quantum reality I call neorealism. Neorealists claim that the familiar objects that make up the everyday world are themselves made of ordinary objects; they believe, in short, that atoms are "things."

Nick Herbert, *Quantum Reality: Beyond the New Physics*

I COME TO THE POETRY READING
WEARING MY NEW SILVER SHOES

for Clayton Eshleman

Listening has many foci: a sunburst locust tree loaded with
    pods.
I look down at my silver shod feet.
They are new stars humming with places to go.

The man with black hair, Groucho Marx glasses and
    cerebral palsy
who snores in his wheelchair so loud
the room is buzzing: he's already gone.
He's prehistoric ape man,
unawakened, dreaming,
wanting to *Make* something, wanting to

articulate, but with hands
that don't coordinate/cooperate.

And the mother with her two young children
sitting in the front row
disrupting the music with little-child
sounds, with crackling paper, with dropping crayons
or pens, and constant movement,
the one little girl drawing pictures and constantly trying to
        draw
our attention.
The mother picks up,
shushes,
puts down,
holds, but surely herself
never has a moment for art,
for crescendo and climax,
when the antiphonal energy of word and voice
surround her
and draw her out of herself completely.
If she could have no pleasure while tending these children,
if the man in the wheelchair snores through the whole
        hour,
why did they come? Surely not to disturb
and annoy the rest of the audience?

They've come, as we all have,
so that you will transform yourself
into the Dancing Sorcerer
and lead us to magic,
Clayton,
they were there as ghosts from Lascaux
and Le Tuc D'Audoubert, the Mother-nipples
hanging from the ceiling of the front row
to remind of primal fertility, the fallen
hunter slumped in his wheelchair with snores
coming out of him like an erect penis, dead

but worshipping your voice and words in his
unconscious, inarticulate body, where a trapped spirit
needs to emerge forward into man's world.

All of us were fuming at those annoying ancestral presences,
transforming the Tower Room into a cave, the words even,
farther away from us, that we have to wiggle down
            towards, crawl on our bellies
and contort our muscular, non-spelunking bodies to get to.

You, standing humbly with big belly and wide lips
ringing out, word after word—   bong

                              bong

                              bong,

                                    bel canto
strikes against the schist and tangled rocks.
The snore finally stops you.
The children exit for a short time,
and we all knit together, trying to reach the cave
where the recognizable bison
are mating.
My silver shoes glow as I walk through your tunnel,
Art is not easy, words are not there
to soothe wild beasts, or music to make
us be seduced or go to sleep. We wiggle and squirm and
            finally reach
the clear wide opening where Gladys
is lying in her caving-in coffin,
and talking to little Clayton, rattling his crayons and paper,
            while Ira
Clayton continues to fuss from his inefficient grave chair.
The voices now seem central
to everything,
and for one sapphiric moment glow

blue-black, even starry. You led us
into the room in the cave
where things began, where Clayton was born from
Gladys' old 38-year body.
Donald Duck is far away,
but we are closer to him than Disney World ever brought
        us, ready to
follow a Dancing Sorcerer home,
to get into the pearl-dark Packard or Buick with him,
with the Dancing Sorcerer sitting behind
the wheel of the car,
wearing his antlers,
owl eyes staring into winter's night,
his wolf tail under him on the American vinyl seats.
He will drive us home, his bear paws square
on the wheel, steering us. Through darkness.
On this snowy midwestern evening.
  "Where is Clayton now," we ask this shaman

as he lets us out, by the side of the house.
But the Dancing Sorcerer backs down the driveway
without a word, and we are left with nothing
but the image of an antlered head
driving away on Division Street.
I walk into my house, kick off my new silver shoes
and leave them, twinkling by the door,
two stars that have just dropped out of the new
evening sky.

SHAPE SHIFTING

"You see, Oz is a great Wizard and can take on any form he wishes. So that some say he looks like a bird; and some say he looks like an elephant; and some say he looks like a cat. To others he appears as a beautiful fairy, or a brownie, or any other form that pleases him. But who the real Oz is, when he is in his own form, no living person can tell."

Frank Baum, *The Wizard of Oz*

DEER GODS

Driving past the thick forested land
next to cherry orchards, loaded with red fruit,
watching for deer, we think we see one
silhouetted against a bend in the road,
but as we approach, we see that it's the shape
of a mailbox post which formed an optical illusion.
But we all saw it, and when we mention it to
neighbors, they know exactly which mailbox it is:
just from a certain distance, the angle of shadows
seems to freeze a deer against the forest dark.

I am sure now that the man I thought I saw
on my fire escape that first year I lived in
New York City, the one which made me scream out
so loud my neighbor got out his gun and shot
into the courtyard, thirty years ago—I am
sure that he was also
an optical illusion, for no one
was in that closed courtyard, and I don't
believe the myths of Alfred Hitchcock movies
about cat burglars, thieves who can slide in and out
of shadows, fade into nothing or night, invisible,
but I do know that we animate the world
and give spiritual life to empty forms
because we need the drama.

Art. How can abstraction offer
any human pleasure. Forms are power.
Even primitive humans knew this.

It is the way we shape angles, curves,
straight lines and circles into
forms which resemble complex
living things that removes us from
our animal past.
   The first man drawing a buffalo
   on the wall of a cave, rather than just eating it and going
   to sleep. In dreams we know that each time
we reshape a thing, it gathers power, and
to make *is* richer than
to be. Still, I wonder why I needed to see an intruder
on my New York City balcony, and if
that mailbox owner knew
when he nailed those timbers together
and positioned them in just such a shape,
holding the tin mailbox, against the bend in the road
that everyone who drove past would see a deer
limned against the woods?

And if, in knowing this,
he was calling for something which could never come to
          him
in the mail, something which was so much bigger, more
powerful than the actual deer who wandered that land,
crossing the road to the cherry orchards and then back
wandering down to the Lake as big as an ocean, their
          delicate toed
tracks leaving evidence they'd come down to drink at night
when no one was looking for them. Did I want to call
forth some spirit of my past, refresh it, make it grow
larger than my life, knowing that to make
something might be a means of remaking
myself? What I should have seen
on my city balcony was a man wearing
the horns of a deer, hollow-eyed mask of antlered head
gazing through my open window, instead of just
a man, anonymous, without description.

52

I should have seen my destiny even,
or a snake hissing there, its white mouth open
like a flower against the bank of a river.

So the Scarecrow followed him and was admitted into the
great Throne Room, where he saw, sitting on the emerald
throne, a most lovely Lady. She was dressed in green silk
gauze and wore upon her flowing green locks a crown of
jewels. Growing from her shoulders were wings, gorgeous in
color and so light that they fluttered if the slightest breath of
air reached them.

Frank Baum, *The Wizard of Oz*

BUTTERFLIES ARE SHADOW SHAPES

The stars are flying
like butterflies.
In the morning,
they hover around the flowers' lips.

I can't find any reason
to learn the shapes
of the constellations,
as their shapes almost never
seem obvious, and often don't relate
to their names. Ursa Major

doesn't look like a bear,
though it does look like a big dipper
which is what it can be called, but is not
what it is named. There's nothing
consistent about constellations. All the
stories which accompany the names
of the constellations seem
to indicate that getting into the sky
could be either a reward
or a punishment, winning or losing,
a way of keeping something in sight,
or a way
of getting rid of it. In other words,
these stories don't make
any more sense than the reputed shapes
and their often unrelated names.

I find myself thinking
    of butterflies
    which I loved so much as a child. I also
    loved horses and the idea
    of Egypt. My private memory bank
is filled with unrelated images.
Does that mean the history of the sky
is a reflection of the way
my mind works?
I remember Swallow Tails,
Monarchs, and Cabbage Butterflies.

Although the world once appeared to be twofold, made of
particles and fields, closer observation reveals a common
behavior. Former "particles" now show their wave aspects;
former "waves" behave like particles. In reality everything is

made of the same kind of substance, which I call quantum-stuff. Quantum theory reflects this fundamental unity of being by describing all quons the same way. One description fits all.

Nick Herbert, *Quantum Reality: Beyond the New Physics*

FRIGHTENING GREEN

It's not enough to know
the leaves do not hide snakes
or hands which reach out to bruise you. It's
not enough
to know the green woods won't keep you
from breathing.

I love the desert where at least you have the illusion
you can see for miles, that nothing can sneak up
on you. Walking is not a foray into
decaying matter, and if there are snakes their girth
can be heard or seen
from a distance; stay away from the rocky
canyons, the holes and caves where predators
disguise their singing with wind and echo.

I hate the telephone lines which tangle out away from me,
like writhing waving cobras, the Medusa's head a
        mouthpiece
turning me to stone, my heavy body mirrored
against beauty. In my drab world, I'm safe.
The silence protects me. Even color

is frightening, though I dream of the red cardinal
bursting into the landscape,
or a flower like a yellow china cup
blooming full on the snakeskin opuntia
which normally blends into the desert,
keeps you away with its thorns.

It's not enough to know
that leaves are innocent. I don't believe,
if I lived on the desert, I would long
for their lush, frightening, heavy green.

"Some physicists would prefer to come back to the idea of
an objective real world whose smallest parts exist objectively
in the same sense as stones or trees independently of whether
we observe them. This however is impossible."

Werner Heisenberg, quoted in
Nick Herbert, *Quantum Reality: Beyond the New Physics*

"Only a mouse!" cried the little animal indignantly. "Why I
am a Queen—the Queen of all the field mice!"

Frank Baum, *The Wizard of Oz*

SIZE

for Steelman

matters to me. I like men who are large as angels,
I like them with flaring cobra shoulders or python arms,
to hold me as if they are chairs or fathers. Sometimes
I am distracted by eyes, or
bones snaking in the face, tight legs
like cowboy singers, or baseball glove hands;
but then it happens. Always ungainly,
I slip, nearly fall,
      or awkwardly knock against a door,
            say, in passing
maybe
      he has to catch me
             by surprise. The arms are there
saving me, and while he might be
an angel,
suddenly I am the one
             with giant spreading wings.

Dear Jonathan,

With your novel, *From the Teeth of Angels*, this year
you have finally broken some of the American
barriers which seem to be set against shaman writers

of fiction. Poets, of course, have never suffered from this prejudice. In fact, we are supposed to be shamen. Few of us are, though Judith Minty and Jerome Rothenberg are two quite authentic magician-poets.

Judith has continued to inspire me with her animal totems and her goddess wisdom that allows me to understand or, at least, accept shape shifting. I guess angels are the primary shape shifters in our modern Western culture. At any rate, I have been fascinated with the frequent appearance of the word "angel" in every aspect of our contemporary lives even before I learned the title of your wonderful book.

Recently, one of my students came up with the phrase "angel wire" to describe a girl's hair. I suppose because of a year's worth of angel thoughts, I heard it as an inspired phrase, though the poem he wrote didn't really use the image of angel wire, or develop it. Because I lingered over the phrase so long, another student suggested that I take up the challenge of using it myself. I imagine it fascinated me so much because, to me, "angel wire" meant something entirely different from hair. For my generation, a "wire" is a telegram.

Yr Lady Who Wants Telegrams From Angels,

DW

ANGEL WIRE OR RECEIVING A SURPRISE RESURRECTION TELEGRAM FROM STUDENT ANGELS ON THE OCCASION OF AUTUMN JUST BEFORE MY HUSBAND DISMANTLES OUR GARDEN

with thanks to Anthony La Penna,
whose phrase it is, and Israel Vines
who suggested I co-opt it for my own
shape shifting purposes. Note: to my
WW II-babies-generation, a "wire"
meant a telegram

You don't expect either
taxis or telegrams, but
as if Henry Miller,
delivering a Cosmodemonic telegram
   for Tom, or someone who might become famous,
had jumped out of bed to stand
on your doorstep,
you open the door.
No one is
there.

A yellow cab driven by someone named Sasha
is speeding away with two
angels sitting on the roof, hanging on
like winding sheets
flapping in a gale. You don't now why
they need to hitch such a breezy ride, and you're not sure
if they are male or female,

or even if they have
wings. Perhaps, like Rob, they have simply
fallen out of a tree.

Heavenly Blue.
Heavenly Blue morning glories. Your whole front garden
was covered with them
this year. Yes, you've been talking
through the seasonal blanket of
flower trumpets so brilliant they might wake up
Miles Davis, but you never thought
the wake-up call
would summon angels to your autumn door.
Everything in the garden bed is darkening to purple and gold,
heavenly, dazzled as Matt's "honey brass woman,"
contrasting with the still-summer-green tall basil
    pointing its long end-of-term lavender tassels like a taxi
        dancer,
    and the pillowy oregano
    relaxing into nippled grape-like furled blossoming.

The sunflowers in the
front yard are
so heavy, their heads hang down
almost to the ground, bowed, as if they are praying
before October's altar or waiting to be buried, resigned
to winter's marriage bed.
    Heather is there too, and she is not

just a common
shrub, she is part of the autumn's
purple, a bedspread
covering the moors
    she and Emily have never seen.

The secret Emily knew,
that only after death can she marry the lover

she longs for:
　　have we discovered that yet?

You've been waiting for
a message; you've heard rumors that
something is about
to happen;
you know something good
is promised because you just opened
what some women might call a jewel box, your
Emerald Garden of puzzles,
and found along with Neale's Baltic amber and your
freshwater pearls
a thin twist of gold wire you're sure
was not there
before.

You had no idea
what it was, thought it might be
a copperhead tendril from the summer's massive show of
morning glories, winding their way even
into the house, though it was silky
and flexible, and sinuous as thread that might have been
used to hold a key around M.J.'s neck when
she was a little latchkey child.

But then the doorbell rang, and you saw
the angels hanging on to the taxicab
as it peeled away, and you knew it wasn't flowers
they'd delivered.
It must be angel wire;
they'd put it there, meant for you
to use it like a telegram, an urgent message,
　　• a wire from Bukowski, Yeats or maybe even Emily
　　　Dickinson—
containing good news
about resurrection,

come beyond the trumpet flower and their
secrets, come as a golden snake, an octave, a ribbon
of keys, a gold
piano wire,
lying coiled there in
your Emerald City tangle,
the string for
a harp on which to play,
an angel wire from Troy, telegraphing
autumn's golden-as-effervescent-lager
news: not "a child is born,"
but "there's a whole classroom
of angels, waiting to spread their wings
on Diane's doorstep today."

Glory, glory.

CRAIG'S HUMMINGBIRDS

for Chris Mandenberg

They move so fast, their motion is invisible.
As color is only light waves, the iridescent red and green
I associate with their plumage might be created by
their motion, and in a mirror a hummingbird might appear
        to be
different colors altogether, as the glass captures even more
of the light. You said,
    "if there were mirrors, I wouldn't be there."

And looking at your tall cowboy-hatted beauty
I smiled. I who have only a misty shadow in mirrors

would surround myself with their glitter and reflections of
    light.
I would look at my body, my face, from every angle,
    searching
for something which might be invented with a different
    length of light;
but you whom both men and women see as beautiful,
you wouldn't study T'ai Chi if it were taught in a room with
mirrors, you said. And I believe you.

I know the secret, that you
are a twin, and all the doubles
which many of us think we long for,
have ganged up on you and made you not even
want to see yourself reflected, for fear it might be that other,
the one whom you reflect but in fact contradict
in every way but image.
You think he will steal you, not just
your soul, as mirrors are thought to steal
the souls of primitive observers,
but you. He will take you,
mimic you, reduce you to parody.

Perhaps you know secrets, but I am the woman,
  holding a rose and the crystal,
  mirroring my Pythoness oracles.
Once I said that I was
afraid of looking into your eyes,
as if I would fall into them and disappear,
but I was lying. I'd already looked into them and seen
    beauty,

the way someone sees God and builds a whole religion
    around
not saying his name, because to say it could never live up to
    God's immensity,
his power. I saw something bigger than the world

when I looked into your unreflected eyes, and now I offer
    you
a lens where you can
also look as long as you need;
you won't find your twin there, or anything but
unshattered light. This mirror does not offer family, or sex,
money or power. It offers only truth, which like Craig's
    hummingbirds,
moves so fast it might be invisible.

One difference between human twins and a pair of photons
in the twin state is that before conception the human twins
are nonexistent, while before measurement the photons
already exist. We know that they were emitted at a certain
time from their source and are traveling with a certain
velocity toward their respective detectors.

Nick Herbert, *Quantum Reality: Beyond the New Physics*

Dear Jonathan,

Last night I watched a Spanish film, *Oriana*, made by
a woman director, which I browsed onto in the
video store. I am not sure why I checked it out,
since it was described as a very "poetic" film, and I
hate so-called poetic novels, films, art in general.
And it wasn't some classic that I heard others talking

about or read about and thought I ought to see for my education. I just checked it out for some mysterious reason.

There are so few films left which I haven't seen at least once, and there is something about watching a film for a second time or reading a book for a second time which I still find irritating. I always want something new. I think the reason I was such an unsuccessful English major was that I hated to read anything more than once. Now, of course, I read many things again, watch films again, but it is because I have developed a bit of the scholarly mind, a bit of the discipline which, along with intuitive genius, creates serious thinkers. I am fast, quick and have spent my life with things which I immediately know, learn, absorb, having no patience for anything which I can't immediately do. This is why my sticking to the beginning T'ai Chi class is so important: that I am trying to learn something which I find beautiful but which is very hard for me.

This film, *Oriana*, is in fact a story about brother-sister incest, beautiful and slow and haunting. The kind of story I like with much search, much looking, much longing, and even the fulfillment full of disaster and difficulty. It's about secrets but more important, the private artistic sharing of secrets with which primary fulfillment comes when an audience, a viewer, another participant, though one who is more voyeur than participant, engages in unearthing the secret and bringing it to some kind of conclusion. The film has a very low rating in my movie book, and its synopsis which I didn't read until I finished watching the film actually misstates the plot. I.e. the reviewer didn't understand what happened. This is the first Spanish film I have ever seen that I liked (so far as I can recall), and I don't think I can watch it again right away because it is a slow film and only keeps you watching to find out what's going on. But I need to watch it again to catch what the director is doing in the way of revealing more about the main character who is the discoverer, not the participant in the incest story.

You know these brother–sister teenage dramas enthrall me, they represent the deepest psychological patterns in my make-up I am sure. I sometimes wonder why Medea became so important to me, since to my knowledge there is no incest in her story at all. Though maybe there is in older versions. Maybe the great taboo is that Jason was her brother? Sent away at birth, now returning to claim the Golden Fleece which he thinks should be his? Might be an interesting thesis for a Classical scholar? I suppose if I were a Classics expert, I wouldn't even suggest such an idea.

At any rate, *Oriana* affected me deeply, and I believe seeing it is what brought me vivid dreams this morning. I say this morning, because I woke up (as usual) around 4 a.m. (when I wake up at night that's when I wake up and get up to go to the bathroom) and when I came back to bed, since I haven't had insomnia this week (Contac drugged sleep, I imagine), I thought I would instantly fall asleep. But I didn't. I lay there for a while, and just as I was thinking "Oh, no, do I have it?" I must have fallen asleep because my next memory is Robert's alarm going off at 8, and waking to the vivid memory of this dream:

I was somewhere in a kind of wooded and shore-like location (Venezuela in the film) but my usual house of many rooms was in the dream, divided as always into two parts, one beautiful and one shabby/as always connected but not connecting except through a bedroom or someone's private space which one wouldn't want to pass through. Only this time the whole house, both parts, were empty, though I realize now that I didn't go into the house until midway in the dream, and I am not sure why I was in it, except that it represented several groups of people who all lived in this various and divided dwelling. The central incident in the first half of the dream which included the house was that we were all outside at a kind of picnic and I held a monkey (! ! !) on my lap and it pissed on me, wrecking my beautiful dress and leaving a horrible stench. At first I mixed this up with buying a lotto or keno ticket and seeing the winning numbers posted in front of all of us on the main table, but not being able to read them. When an old but beautifully made-up woman, like a movie star in her 70s, Billie Burke (as Glinda the Good?) or some bejeweled type of actress, came over to me and brought me to the table, and I thought it was because my ticket had the winning number, but it turned out to be that she was trying to assist me in getting rid of the foul-smelling dress with the monkey piss on it. She helped me discard it into a straw basket, like a big purse or suitcase, and we left it there. I felt confused because I had mixed up my lotto ticket with the big wet yellow piss stain on my dress. There was a section of the dream, perhaps in the next part but I don't remember, when I was carrying the straw case with the foul-smelling dress in it and it was so awful that I had to find water and rinse and rinse and rinse it so that the smell didn't attach itself to me (Lady Macbeth?).

Then in the second part of the dream I was walking with a group of young people. I think I looked young but I knew that I was my Diane-age. Two of the young men drew me off and we walked together ahead of the others. One of them seemed like my twin, or had some relationship to me, and he was dark and beautiful like the boy in *Oriana*. He put his arm around me and I can't remember what happened but this is when I knew that all the rooms of the house were empty, even though we had been on the wooded shore walking together. Then he seemed to disappear and the other boy/man put his arm around me, and I seemed to be covered with grapes or berries, or maybe they were a necklace around his bare upper torso. I felt so healed with just his touch. He was my friend, and I knew he could be my lover if I wanted him to be. But I just walked with him. I somehow knew I was too old to be his sexual partner, but it didn't seem to matter, he loved me. He held me just walking together with me, his arms around me. I woke up feeling almost dizzy with some kind of connection, erotic, though not really sexual. The kind I talk about in my poems so much.

I suppose I should attribute this dream also a bit to a science fiction novel I read yesterday by wonderful Walter Tevis (*The Hustler* author, but need I tell you since your father wrote the film script for that movie?). A friend just sent me three more Walter Tevis books which I hadn't previously seen or read. One, a famous novel, *The Man Who Fell to Earth*, also science fiction, is a great book. This one, *Mockingbird*, is about a futuristic world where it is against the law to read and in fact no one even knows that because no one knows what reading is! But the main character discovers secretly hidden books and learns to read, and thus the story begins. *Mockingbird* is one of the best books I have ever read about how important reading and writing and the life of the mind, which is connected to these two acts, are. It made me want to make all my students read the book before they ever stepped into my classroom. I think it's out of print, but I have to check that some time and see what I can do. Maybe the effect will wear away in the next few months, and I will just think of it as another good novel, but yesterday it had me racing.

Yes, somehow the erotic part of my dream I associated with reading!

Yr Lady of Duality,

DW

MAGIC BOOKS

In 1932 von Neumann set down his definitive vision of quantum theory in a formidable tome entitled *Die Mathematische Grundlagen der Quantenmechanik*. Our most general picture of quantum theory is essentially the same as that outlined by von Neumann in *Die Grundlagen* (The Foundations). Von Neumann's book is our quantum bible. Like many other sacred texts, it is read by few, venerated by many.

Nick Herbert, *Quantum Reality: Beyond the New Physics*

KELLY AS THE MAGE

Remember when I came to Brooklyn
and helped you pack your books? You
had a bedroom full of bears.
It was before your first wife
had cancer, when you
were both young and fat.
And I was slim
and serious.

Like a little bunch of green grapes.

California.
I must have had it written
on the arch of my
white foot.
Stars on my fingers
and The Pony Express Rider escorting me
along Manhattan streets, before I even really
knew—I must have known/but certainly didn't
        understand—
that men could love other men. I guess I thot
that ultimately they must
love women. You'd think, growing up with women,
hating the women's world as I did, I would have figured out
that some men never do.

Before epidemic AIDS. Before you got thin and became a
        Buddhist.
Before any of us thought of old age or pensions,

though you were already teaching in a college.
I was living
for Art. Never got
enough sleep
when I worked 48 hours a week. Hardly
could pay my rent either.
Before lofts were legal in New York
or there was a SoHo, to say nothing of a TriBeCa
or Yuppies.

Remember how I believed that you had to control
the physical in order to
reach the spiritual? Oh, little white-footed Berkeley girl
remembering her black-leather-jacketed motorcycle poetry
        teacher
and talking so seriously in coffee houses and cheap
Greek or Indian restaurants.

I was young.
Serious.
Tight as a green grape.
So serious.

I never understood your interest
in the Devil.
You were Catholic. No wonder I tantalized you
with my deck of tarot cards, my Mary Magdalene history
and my pure white feet. If I hadn't come to Brooklyn after
work that night and helped you pack your books—50
        cartons
full—would you and Joby ever have reached
Annandale-on-Hudson?

Of course. But perhaps there would be nothing else to say
about me when I die, or nothing so telling. Now you can
        say,
"She once helped me

pack all my books. It seemed hopeless.
The bedroom was full of bears.
The dust of Brooklyn, like cement.
She loved touching books,
having them around her. She worked then
in a bookstore. I haven't seen her now for
many years."

You'll be 95, and I
93. This is what poetry is for:
to predict the future,
to chain ourselves with the only chains we ourselves can
        forge,

a linking of vowels, of consonants, of
sounds never beyond language, though
not always understood.

Kelly, remember what we shared?

The mystery of black words on white paper.
Boxes full. Cartons and cartons full.
Moving from your dusty apartment in Brooklyn
to the country landscape of Alexander Hamilton,
Revolutionary troops, British generals.
Moving your books,
not knowing which ones might really have

every secret
printed on their crumbling pages.

LIGHT

I live for books
and light to read them in.
  Water lilies

reaching up
from the depths of the pond
algae dark,
the frog loves a jell of
blue-green water,
  the bud

scales
a rope of stem,
then floats in sunshine. Like soap
in the morning bath.

This book I read
floats in my hand like a water lily
coming out of the nutrient waters
of thought
and light shines on us both,
the morning's breviary.

WAITING FOR JASON

A Meditation on the Motorcycle Betrayer

White lady★
like a narcissus
between the pages of
a book, before he had totally
   rejected her,

   betrayed her.

She told him
trees frightened her,
out of Tolkien, the living branchy
hands and roots of Tom Bombadil's forest,
trees grasping her, strangling her,
leaving her trapped and floating
like a log in the swamp. When tall,
their murmuring rustle, the leaves
touching each other paperishly,
they seemed like snakes whispering over sand.
Waiting, gossiping,
sparrows at our summer feeder
opium and girls,
card tables, gambling, death,
white ladyness.

★*In Breton folklore and fairy tales, the white ladies appear as kind of ghostly figures which herald death, perhaps are there to lead you to the land of the dead. They are not usually seen by anyone except those who are going to die or who have the faerie gifts.*

No longer a sorceress.
Youth.
Wrong choices.
Jason.
Old Medea.
White lady, at the edge of the garden,
Luxor, the glass city of Oz, her desert? straw-
berries, caviar, chocolates, hot blintzes.

EMERALD CITY

This is the green place,
and under my pillow I hide the book
which records the ivory name.

No bones in it,
easy to tell the wrong story.
I'd set fire under
her feet, I'd call you
from a phone booth hidden
in my palm.

I'd go to the sunset beach,
on the boulevard of palms,
I'd ask for a ride
from the man in leathers,
I'd eat an orange
and then play cards all night.

You can't tell me anything
which will make the burning stop,
but I can offer an emerald to
cool it, an ivory stylus to write with.

I go to sleep every night
with the book on fire under my
pillow, but you don't know
the degree of heat it takes to press
emeralds, you don't know
why I love the desert, yet
stay in the green place.
What you don't know about me
would fill a book.

FOR LINDA'S MOTHER

So you read a Diane Wakoski book
of poems and saw *Jean de Florette*
all in the same year, your sixtieth,
and oh, is your family worried, this nice
housewifely woman, soaking up art
like a sponge, bathing in it like Elizabeth Taylor,
energetically dancing it as if John Travolta
were your new partner.

It's not that we come to art   only
when we don't have the press of
children, tedious or strenuous jobs,
have "free time," or as we metaphorically say,
    "time on our hands," as if it were dirt
    or something sticky we need to rub off.
But when the illusion that the body could   ever
satisfy us disappears, or gradually recedes,
we turn to money or art or books
that are not better than our formerly tan
legs or beautiful faces, our children,
our working muscles and strength.

But unlike our children or our bodies
those things will not leave us,
not go away without returning any time
we want to call them back.
How obvious. And how troubling to see
the elderly only knitting for the grandchildren,
or going to the gym, only getting plastic surgery
or buying things/ this   is
the second life any religion
could promise, where the mind
replaces the body. How nice to hear that you are
eating poems instead of cookies, weeping
over a French peasant losing his land
rather than yourself/ not being cheated or tricked
though just as surely,
  losing the ground you thought
  was your life.

Still, I'd say it's not just a landslide, or
an avalanche, but more like the beaches at high tide,
when you think you feel so much sand sliding out from
under your feet that it seems as if
the land will vanish, but then
the tide washes in again, burying your
wet feet in new silica;
old sand eroded,
new sand replaced it:

the even shore remains. That's my interpretation:
time for your family to take off their shoes,
dig their toes into the moving earth!

Once you get down to the quantum randomness level, no further explanation is possible. You can't go any deeper because physics stops here. Albert Einstein, no fan of the orthodox ontology, objected to this fundamental lawlessness at the heart of nature when he said that he could not believe that God would play dice with the universe. This new kind of ultimate indeterminism may be called quantum ignorance: we don't know why an electron strikes a particular phosphor because there's nothing there to know about. When the dice fall from the cup, on the other hand, their unpredictable outcome is caused by classical ignorance—by our unavoidably partial knowledge of their real situation.

Nick Herbert, *Quantum Reality: Beyond the New Physics*

FOR CATHERINE WHO SAYS SHE IS WUTHERING HEIGHTS

Inside the tiny wooden building
where she has a doll-house apartment,
   wearing a long black skirt, her hair tied up
   in a Russian scarf, red roses grounded in black,
she is painting her rooms. A creamy white.
She leaves the doors closed because she doesn't want
anyone to see her, and the windows are closed too
because it is snowing outside. Winter light
is what she wants to recreate on her walls, winter
of brassy samovars and amber tea in glasses,
the sugar cube held between the teeth

which imparts the black hole in the mouths of old men
and women. She has boarded
her cat, her books are covered with translucent plastic
and the sheen of the man-made is filling her nostrils.
New. Fresh. She'll start over. Her memories
of the lusting stepfather, the Russian-eyed mother,
and the lovers who only existed in books or were
anonymous strangers on Greyhound buses,
pool players in bars; her name is Catherine,
and she says
she is Wuthering Heights,
but I say
she has chosen to be Heathcliff, and he is,
we all know,
never rescued, as the women are.

I guess those
Brontë girls all saw each other rescuing themselves
from the dark world, while Branwell, their brother,
drugged and drank
himself beyond possibility.
But this is the trouble with shaping your
life out of literature. You can be
anything you choose, but what if you choose
the wrong book, or the wrong character? I am drawing this
        image,
as she is painting her apartment
because I can't help her, I can't rescue her, I
can't turn her into Catherine or even Heathcliff,
rather than that cold gloomy house on the moors where
        nothing good
can happen; nor can I change her
into Emily or Charlotte rather than Branwell,
or even into a modern woman not wracked with paranoiac
        fears.
I wish she could put on a long black cloak
and go walking on the heath, carrying a loaf of parkin

a bit of cheese and an apple in her pockets.
   Carry a

copy of *Wuthering Heights*, if she wanted to,
and sit sheltered from the wind and read it
while eating her satisfying coarse lunch,
her black-stockinged legs sprawled comfortably against
the gorse-covered hill. Read it again, realizing
that she could be a woman,
   that women rescue

themselves/in the Brontë novels.
That she does not need
to start a new life,
only to claim the power
of her old one.

One of the inevitable facts of life is that all of our choices are real choices. Taking one path means forsaking all others. Ordinary human experience does not encompass simultaneous contradictory events or multiple histories. For us the world possesses a singularity and concreteness apparently absent in the atomic realm. Only one event at a time happens here; but that event really happens.

Nick Herbert, *Quantum Reality: Beyond the New Physics*

PARKIN*

Simple bread for tea. Oh think of those mornings
of early rising, the coke fire to be built in the grate; think
of the skirts of soft muslin, over petticoats that drape
softly around plump bodies; oh think of the Yorkshire
    moors
which were as green as new onions,
  open and damp,
  held the spirit's desire for freedom
where Wesley's religion flourished as did the fantasies
of love that girls like the Brontës cherished.
Men were the prisons,
and the prisoners,
and men who didn't want to be
became
the worse imprisoned, Branwell
  covering his pain with laudanum.

I saw those small rounded loaves, sitting
in the bakery window, just
the size of the clay circles
  in which we, in kindergarten, imprinted our hands,
  clay circles sent off to be baked
  in a kiln and glazed (mine was green and shiny,
  like a new spring rhododendron leaf)
and I, always the scholar of new foods,
rolled the name around my tongue for an entire day:
"parkin, parkin, parkin," imagining

*Parkin is a kind of gingerbread, made in small loaves and eaten as bread rather
than a dessert. It is a common local food in England's Brontë country.

84

I would wear my black woolen cloak swirled around me
for a tramp onto the heath, and carry in a large pocket
underneath the cloak, a loaf of parkin, an apple, a bit of
  cheese.
I didn't know what it tasted like, until tea time, when I ate
half a mince pie, hot and sweet,
and a bit of parkin—oh gingerbread,
slightly chewy just blunted with a little molasses,
the energy of it would wave through you
as you walked in the damp cold, seeing a world

of ups and smooth downs.
I imagined
  one of the girls
  pulling it out of the oven early in the morning, and the
    smell of it
  coming up through the stairway to my bedroom
  where I was still snuggled and bundled into the covers of
    night,
  with a steaming pot of tea on the table next to the bed,
    the fire in the grate lit
for me by some earlier riser. So small, these comforts:
the fire, the tea, the parkin, then the freedom of the walk.
But everything, when you consider the human condition,
    everything,
  when you consider war, or famine, or urban poverty, or
    torture.

Forget about love and its absence, or lack of recognition
for your work. Forget about unsympathetic relatives or
    boring
jobs and daily life. Remember these
small things
as everything.

"Grateful," don't be grateful.
Such a chore.

Just remember
the small things: the parkin, the fire in the grate,
the cup of tea, the walk on the moors, or even this great
comfort, sitting here with words,
   with the yew bushes in the Michigan backyard
   covered with pillowy snow, the bird feeder abandoned by
      even
   our unshowy birds, but now filled,
    a small thing,
   waiting for the cardinals and the blue jays and infinite
      flocks of sparrow
   to discover we're back and offering
    the small things,
   cracked sunflower seeds
   ("50 pounds of oilers," I hear the clerk say).
Everything
has its vocabulary.
Another small pleasure.
Sally's voice from out of the Pacific, dripping with plum
      jam
"remember the small things, the cup of tea..."

I've remembered, thought, about them as we walked
in Haworth village,
ate parkin, as we've come home
to our small lives and the small things,
the small things
which save us from
desolation.

TEA CEREMONY

The blue jay
swaying on the head
of the sunflower,
jabbing at seeds, as he swings.

UNPERMITTED SILENCE

We
old desert rats
are used to it.
Even the rattler keeps still
unless he's annoyed,
angry,
ready to get you.
But stillness,
silence,
unpermitted, as we
eat with our friends.

The birds all dive
for the feeder chirping. I think
it's warning to others, not to
grab their targeted perches.
If, as the dieters say, "parties are for friends,
not food," then I too

should not find this talk so much a chore.
No wonder my friends
think I'm odd;
no sense of rhythm and flow.
A desire for only books,
the words rehearsed and prepared.
Music is always outside of language.
While I listen
for the missing chord,
it is the listening, not the hearing,
that I do best.

Until recently the sound of music was restricted to tonal qualities that could be produced by instruments which actually exist. Now Fourier's theorem provides the method and cheap transistor oscillators provide the means for the creation of entirely new tone colors—sounds impossible to produce by mechanical means.

Nick Herbert, *Quantum Reality: Beyond the New Physics*

DESERT NOSE

No way to look
at Black Hawk Island,
twenty-five years after the poet's★ death

★*Lorine Niedecker*

with its spring flooded road
and not think of a life where the smell
of damp, or of dry rot, molding carpet,
warped pages of books
would not be a daily smell.

My desert nose
wants water to be scarce
and as fragrant
when it comes, as a woman's
lingerie drawer, but I admire the dryness
of language, generated in this fecund place, as a
balance to its never-drying landscape.

The hawk's nest high and dry
in bare branches. She
writes a poem
to raise her roof.

Now the Wicked Witch of the West had but one eye, yet
that was as powerful as a telescope, and could see everything.

Frank Baum, *The Wizard of Oz*

MALACHITE

or marble,
polished like apples

she selects a globe
don't touch, spinning
in angel light,
her fingers gold cylinders.

No one can read this name
written in the emerald book.

I think it is the name of a child
who was found under an apple tree
a green blanket wrapped around his
silvery hands, a sandaled foot
slipped away, not Sappho, someone with
an arrow behind her shoulder.

I can read the name;
I know what it says.
It says "Put on your glasses,
then open this book of malachite
and read river water,
read lily stems,
read frogskin." And somewhere
in those instructions the arrow
comes whizzing out and strikes you.

Green light, malachite/ it could be

marble, polished like apples
this message trembles
like peonies in the rain.

MAGIC FLOWERS

On and on they walked, and it seemed that the great carpet of deadly flowers that surrounded them would never end.

... great clusters of scarlet poppies, which were so brilliant in color they almost dazzled Dorothy's eyes.

"Aren't they beautiful?" the girl asked, as she breathed in the spice scent of the flowers.

"I suppose so," answered the Scarecrow. "When I have brains I shall probably like them better."

Frank Baum, *The Wizard of Oz*

SUMMER LIGHT

So now it's the reds
which are glowing, in the whiskey barrel tub,
like Robert's shoulders when he comes in
from working all afternoon
in the
sun.
Impatiens, and I dreaming of a salad
with crisp arugula, some Bibb lettuce, and nasturtium
flowers, also red, perhaps with yellow throats, a
smudge of black, yes, like the markings on a pansy,
another flower, rich purple this one, with a yellow throat also
which could be tossed on top of this salad.

How I long to eat flowers
everyday/ remember with tenderness
the evening by the Pacific Ocean in Malibu
with Craig when he was thin, and beautiful Cynthia
who has gone away—the yucca bell flowers
on top of our salads

like eating the beauty
we see in women, without marring it
or touching it, or having to witness
withering, wrinkling skin.
I could live my life just thinking
of the petals of flowers.

VIOLETS

cups of them
the wet bank, earth cressed,
roots exposed in the cutaway grainy
crust

water tears at the edges,
but the violets on the bank
near a tree are firm,
not fragile, even resist sometimes
the crushing of a foot, springing back
as if they could not so easily be
torn or pressed away.

The candied violets with which I've
adorned chocolate glazed tortes
stay fresh for years. So that we forget
it was not the sweet which we sugared them for,
but age. The natural taste of violets
or pansies reminding your mouth of hummingbird life
bee genes, ant activity, spilled honey.

The lion man said to us he didn't know if he'd like

eating flowers. I smiled to myself, thinking
that he'd probably eaten hundreds
and not known it. Anyone who drinks tea,
has drunk flowers; pea pods often flourish the vestige
of the white flower at their tips; the world is studded
with rose petals. Jasmine, chamomile, saffron,
nasturtium: surely these petals or stamens
have passed his lips some time?

I think he must have had an image of a cattleya
massively presented, like a steak on his place. Or a giant
lily being offered in someone's hand, to hold and crunch
    on.
The smallness of so many flowers, edible and otherwise,
might be another reason we don't think of them.
So interesting, then, that this tiny one,
the violet,
commands notice:
La Traviata,
The Fallen Woman,
or the trivial one,
the small one. Her name is
Violetta, pretty woman. How can we forget her
as we sing her name?

"I always did like flowers," said the Lion; "they seem so
helpless and frail. But there are none in the forest as bright as
these."

They now came upon more and more of the big scarlet
poppies and fewer and fewer of the other flowers, and soon
they found themselves in the midst of a great meadow of
poppies. Now it is well known that when there are many of

these flowers together their odor is so powerful that anyone who breathes it falls asleep, and if the sleeper is not carried away from the scent of the flowers he sleeps on and on forever. But Dorothy did not know this, nor could she get away from the bright red flowers that were everywhere about; so presently her eyes grew heavy and she felt she must sit down to rest and to sleep.

Frank Baum, *The Wizard of Oz*

QUEEN ANNE'S LACE

for a Robinson Jeffers daughter-in-law

Broken stems—
you see them in the darkening
November field. The stems of chicory,
mullein, wild carrot, and the stained dark pods
of the milkweed, like rusted machine parts,
sometimes in the morning
gloved with rime, hoarfrost
giving the sodden stalks false
brilliance.

It is so hard to understand sleep,
hard to understand waiting
rather than finality. We do not want,
often, to accept finality, but we have little trouble
actually understanding it. Like a spade
which is denied penetration into frozen winter
ground, the mind becomes

one of those brown stems holding brown emblems
which once were flowers.

Hang on.

Hang on. We're passing the house in Carmel
where he used to live,
lace curtains hide the windows which sparkle
in November light.

She planted, after his death,
  and even though the house
  had become a kind of shrine,
  historians wanted to preserve
  actually, the number and kind of plants
  growing there during
  his lifetime,
she planted
delphiniums, a hybrid
she could previously never afford,
and a purple swallow-colored morning glory, also hybrid,
to climb over the
roof of the cottage and blaze
in an Egyptian splendor which could
never have existed
when he lived;
she planted, expensive as Elizabeth Taylor
scarlet poppies,
and brought the roses to a
level of horticultural excellence not previously
possible; she
planted every Cleopatra color and vibrancy
her life never had
when he lived—old and drunk
most of the time,
a great man, though not really
very popular,

always shunned a little.

Plants remind me
of how plain our daily lives
must be. The effort required, in spite of the Bible,
to make even lilies grow and flourish, produce enough to
        be
abundant, to bring inside.

This man, a
different one,
who puts his eye on one petal
at a time, how can all women not
love him? Petal, I said,
not particle.

You laugh
while I track down
the reference in "Queen Anne's Lace"/
beheaded before winter. In Michigan, these stalks
often stand even into the next year's
renewal. It is neither wave, nor particle,
which makes them never
seem to change. It is not
light, but rather,
our sense
of light.

Of destiny.
Never averted.

CARDINAL AT THE FEEDER

You must have waited for this grey and wet
spring morning. It's such a fine
accessory to your
plumage.

FLOWER PARTS

That's what they look like,
these tubes projected out from
the creamy petal face of the narcissus:
the mouths of children just finishing an orange popsicle.

SKETCHING FLOWERS

When I discovered that my eye
could hold a line, and that I could follow it
with my pen-filled hand, as if I were tracing a map,
only this map led to the petals of
a rose, I suddenly felt as if
I could live a different
life, one more intricate than I had
ever imagined. Imagination:

101

that was my problem. I had believed
in imagination, that in my head were the patterns,
the maps, the designs that I could follow,
free hand, if I just let myself move the pen over the white
thickness of rag or wood pulp. But there
was nothing most of the time, or unrecognizable
—I hardly want to call them—shapes.
If I had an inner eye, it only saw numbers, letters,
and scarcely even fathomed them made out of lines. But my
        poor
outer eye, near-sighted, astigmatic, never perfectly corrected
with compass-thick lenses, why I could focus it
on the center of the unfolding rose! I could perfectly sketch
the first petal, then because I saw the point of connection,
or the moment of contiguous repose, I could liltingly tap the
        pen
and indicate the next petal, and the next, until a rose
bloomed on the paper, and it was like coming to a road
indicated on the map that you had never dreamed was there
until you studied it closely.

I want to live my life
now, as if I were sketching a rose;

I want to look at a pattern somewhere,
start in the center where the fragrance is concentrated,
draw a ruffled line that indicates how furled
the middle still is, work my way out
to bigger and bigger petals, until the whole world
can see that I have created an immaculate rose,
perhaps only in black and white,
with an inexpensive pen.

I want to do that, but first
I have to find the rose,
the one from which to draw my life.

Consciousness-created reality goes one step farther. Consciousness selects (or at least acts as the site for such a selection) which one of the many position possibilities actually becomes realized. Thus the meter option selects what game shall be played (position instead of momentum, for instance); consciousness "creates reality" by deciding what particular attribute shall materialize. (Observer creation of the second kind.)

Nick Herbert, *Quantum Reality: Beyond the New Physics*

NIGHT

Did she ride to you,
or did you dream it?
  "Rose, my name is rose."

But she is not the Rose you
know, with hair dark as roasted chestnuts.

The man I love lives behind
a camera. He sees me in the only light,
the only light.
Emerald Light, Rose Light, Apple Light.
In our summer garden, there is a cup of light,
which winter fills with diamonds.

Rose. Rose.
You are still following her when
she should be following you. Doesn't she know

your knightly arm with golden hairs glistening on it
could pull her out of the tunnel, the forest where she has
        ridden?
Pour a cup of light into her mouth?

Did she ride to you,
or did you dream it?
She is the rose, but
you are the light.

THE ROSY TRICKSTER, OLD COYOTE

What I want to see
is an expanse of the Pacific Ocean,
Paul Newman's black and white "hustler" eyes,
the boy with the black leather jacket and muscles,
a man looking at me in plain sexual desire;

instead, there is an image of myself
disguising her 45-year-old fat.
Past the worst, now
that I'm over fifty.

You've turned fifty too, you write.
Creeley had new babies
at that age, but I am Persephone in winter,
with a rock instead of a pomegranate in my hand/ don't
        look at my
hands, they are the part of me that cannot conceal aging.
From a distance
you might mistake me
for a girl/
it was the girl's mother who went down after her,

weeping, and Kore never really comes back, only
her image.
I am thin again, and from a distance might look like
        Persephone
gathering crocus, their saffron tongues bitter.

It is only now
now that I am older that I have turned
bitter, the word you called me

when I wasn't.
(The best chocolate:
bittersweet.)

The saffron tongues
which you and I will never taste again.

I almost told the secret story
in front of the fire,
saffron tongues flicking back the cold day;
but what is
the story?

A caller to a movie talk show: "What is
the name of the rose? What does that mean?" It's the girl's
        name
being referred to,
that he
even as a priest longs for; but he's
never known her name. She's only
"the rose."
Naming.
Naming is the mystery,
not the passion. Rose, the passion,
the symbol for passion.
"Rosy" crucifixion, to kill
yourself for love. Isn't that

what all of us do?
Sex like snow on a grave,
the saffron-tongued fire snapping at the woman
who believes that I'll change
from the one who descended into the rocky cave and came
      out
a shadow,
who believes that something more substantial
than language anchors us.

I do not accept this.
Somehow I know
we have not been given all
the facts. Some vital piece
of evidence is missing. It is not just
that we do not know "the name of the rose,"
but that we are missing
the tongue, the saffron tongue,
the key to what the rose is, which is not
contained in its name.
   When I disappeared into the rocky tunnel

the only return possible
was a shadow, and it was that
which depended on the name.

She is right;
there is something more substantial than
language.
The rose, itself, deceptively glittering
its lips
rr—rr—rr—rrrrrrrrrrose, Rose, C'est (Selavy) la vie/

il me prend dans ses bras, Duchamp, you

trickster.

On the one side, there is life.
On the other, death.
Which one is
the rose/

        a rose

               by any other

name...

Rose Selavy, have you finally turned fifty too?

Feynman assumes that the unmeasured world works according to two rules:

1. A single quon takes all possible paths.
2. No path is better than any other.

Nick Herbert, *Quantum Reality: Beyond the New Physics*

LILY HANDS

I know this girl must once
have had
two hands like everyone else does,
but today one hand
is a prosthetic device,
not quite a hook, industrial metal buttons
on a tapered bole, When
I see her gesture

with her real hand,
the fingers look long and soft
as the taper of lily buds,
and like a water lily, they are pale as foam
on green waves.
She holds her metal replacement
in her beautiful hand, adjusts the watch band
that is strapped to the place where her
wrist would be, and seems to caress
this non-lily part of her body
adorned with the time piece.
I wriggle my own fingers resting in my lap
with my hands that are spotted with age and
connected to my real arms, thinking
about the morning glories whose vines were so long
and so twisted that they wound round and round
the last of the garden's dahlias
that I picked yesterday
and now sit in crystal, closing at night,
and opening this morning
when the sun touched them. How they
aren't connected anymore to the root or system
that should have given them
open and shut instructions,
wondering how she operates
her mechanical hand
that doesn't look like a hand, or a hook,
but sort of like
a set of elevator buttons.
What opens and closes
the gripping pads she now has?
What makes connections, closes
circuits, helps her wash
the other hand?
        that pale lily
                now holding a replacement
                        for beauty?

WITCHES

"There were only four witches in all the Land of Oz, and two of them, those who live in the North and the South, are good witches. I know this is true, for I am one of them myself, and cannot be mistaken. Those who dwelt in the East and West were, indeed, wicked witches, but now that you have killed one of them, there is but one Wicked Witch in all the Land of Oz—the one who lives in the West."

Frank Baum, *The Wizard of Oz*

AGING

Yes, you could put my entire brain
into a daffodil this morning
and still get a hollow sound
when you blew through its trumpet cup.

ALEXANDER★

When she smooths me and smooths me, as I lie
on the student's table, she is making
the bed of my body, smoothing and smoothing my back;
as if it is a sheet which will not stay unwrinkled in place.
Her hands, like the hands of us all as we age,
are gloved with what they do.

Watching some footage of a medical doctor,
I thought at first he had on surgical gloves, but
it was the onionskin smoothness and the crinkling skin
        tissue
as he dispensed tablets, which simply made
an old man's hands
seem gloved.

★*Alexander work focuses on the body's natural use of gravity to avoid twisted,
stiff and unnatural postures which cause pain as the body is misused over the
years. Many Alexander teachers are musicians, actors, or former dancers, as is
my teacher, Mary Montgomery.*

My own hands
these betrayers which would keep me from ever
again taking
a young lover/ they are gloved with fawn-spotted skin
that forever makes love
an act of the imagination.
Even the word—a lepered touch.

In times of trouble, these folded hands
move up across the chest,
up to the face and clasp themselves
in supplication:
    "Give me peace," or
    "Forgive me,"
    "Make him love me,"
    "Don't let me die."

    Gloved against god,
    or gloved against love,

    or gloved to heal?
My hands are gloved with age,
and when my Alexander teacher lays them folded
on my breast, as she
smooths and smooths my aching shoulders,
helps me to release my neck, moves the hand

and arm up, away from my elder body, a smooth arc,
relaxed, and then back down articulating each
of the fingers as if she is a lover who wants
to know the particular beauty
of these hands, I know she is teaching me
a posture which in its soft infinities
and wavy smoothness, will release me
from pain, give me strength, make
me an object free to be loved,
even though these gloves, the age on my hands,

are the final, natural fence
between what I think
and what I can do.

The modern field concept allows us to regard gravity as a
strictly local interaction even though it acts across vast
reaches of space.

Nick Herbert, *Quantum Reality: Beyond the New Physics*

OUR LADY OF THE CHANTERELLES

for Judith Minty

I love knowing that when a person opens
her hand, there is a map there,
if only you know what to look for. How to read it.

Looking into your American hand, Judith,
I see that you have surveyed San Francisco
and inscribed its arc-ing bridges
as rings on all your fingers.
You're driving your daughter the chef over the Golden
     Gate
into Napa-Sonoma, on your way to white table cloths
and daily roux, drinking those nectar-y chardonnays
and wondering about how much more at home you feel

113

in Northern California, with baskets of chanterelles and
        hedgehogs
rather than the wrinkled brainy morels of your own state.

In the light of chanterelles that twist and crown you,
        Judith,
in Western light glinting from the sharpest knife,
in maplight, and in kitchenlight, together, you and Annie
will eat the bread of Marin County, dipped in green
olive oil and try a risotto cooked with fennel and porcini
        mushrooms,
and think of how the redwoods
of California, and the Douglas firs now
seem part of a Western map both you
and your daughter have on your hands.
The map of Michigan is a mitten, a throwback
to the first opposable thumbs.
No dexterous articulated fingers to accompany them.
No chef's hand so skillfully trained as Annie's; no eye
for beauty
like the one
she gets from you.
And your hands,
    Mother daughter, traveling in mushroom light,

what do they really map or, touching,
see? A dotted road of light,
leading to the center?
Like the illumination that reminds me I am in exile?
Unable, like you, to make two maps, or is it two roads?
turn into one inexorable
set of lines
on my palm?
I could say the map
was too watery here in Michigan,
though there is no Pacific Ocean
with its primal salty broth.

My hand's map seems empty and smooth,
dry as Death Valley.

Our Lady of Chanterelles,
I turn to you. Open your hand: show me the secret,
the beauty of this aging
desolated terrain.

FLOWER MASKS

Snapdragons
next to the parking lot.
Multicolored, like confetti,
when you're far away.
They could be children on the playground
in snowsuits. They could be
the hall closet, when we've left all
our motley of coats and jackets.
But instead, they are just like people,
looking so different from a distance than from
up close. Up close, you open their velvety mouths,
little dragon jaws to slip over a finger in play,
you put them next to your face for their softness
and you look at their furred ridges,
undulating curves, postillioned length.
You know they are silent
when they snap, and they never
do it on their own.

Now you drive away with them scattered
on your retina, masking the reason
you noticed them, masking
the reason you are leaving,
driving away.

What von Neumann showed was that if you assume that electrons are ordinary objects or are constructed of ordinary objects—entities with innate dynamic attributes—then the behavior of these objects must contradict the predictions of quantum theory.

Nick Herbert, *Quantum Reality: Beyond the New Physics*

MASKS

That's all it is—
my aging body—
a mask
covering youth. I used
to think that; though now
when I look at grown but still young
boy/men, women/girls
　I think,

"that skin, those breasts or
legs, or muscles—They're not real. They are
just a mask,
covering your aged body, the real
one you will expose when you are over
fifty." I know this because I
realize there is more need for
beautiful masks than ugly ones,
and I know that what I wear now is not
a cover. This is simply the truth which was masked
by clear skin and firm muscles
when I was young.

Quantum Reality #2: The Copenhagen interpretation, Part II (Reality is created by observation). Although the numerous physicists at the Copenhagen school do not believe in deep reality, they do assert the existence of phenomenal reality. What we see is undoubtedly real, they say, but these phenomena are not really there in the absence of an observation.

Nick Herbert, *Quantum Reality: Beyond the New Physics*

... the Witch Glinda sat upon a throne of rubies.

She was both beautiful and young to their eyes. Her hair was a rich red in color and fell in flowing ringlets over her shoulder. Her dress was pure white but her eyes were blue, and they looked kindly upon the little girl.

Frank Baum, *The Wizard of Oz*

THE BLUE DRESS/AIRMAIL LETTER

At the 66th Academy Awards ceremony, when Deborah Kerr tottered on stage to receive her Lifetime Achievement Award,

117

dressed in voluminous old-lady clothes, a
kind of morning glory blue, with her hair
dyed blond and sprayed into the coif of
expensively cared-for aging women, and
stumbled as she approached the podium,
having to reach for Glenn Close to prevent
herself from falling, I burst into tears. I
realized how much I hate aging, how awful
it is that we get trapped into these old
bodies, and that publicly it might be worse
for a beauty queen or movie star than for
me or any non-celebrity woman, but
privately it is the same. Most of us have
cared about Beauty, about sex, love and
romance with the body, or even about
wholeness that the young body represents
and the old one no longer can claim. She
gave an elegant, gracious acceptance speech,
holding back her own tears, and I simply
cried for a whole minute, out loud, and
desperately. Crying for myself of course.

The old movie star swathed in chiffon, blue as an airmail
    letter,

  artificially golden hair stiff as tissue paper,
  she's winging it,
  almost tottering flimsily,
  on to the Academy Awards stage

stumbles just slightly, but is caught by the firm vellum hand
of a younger actress, who now
over forty has begun to lose
parts to new beauties, but never wavers.

Both retain paper-crisp control
that bends like wings in motion,

118

while I at home, behind my video screen
have started weeping. She stumbled but I fell,
she's still on stage, her old/young images flooding the
     screen,
oh, blue, blue,
her "heavenly blue," morning glory colored dress,
empty sky, angels don't cry,
so much false grief in a little step,
the unmailed letter.

HANSEL AND GRETEL

for Heather Abner

What would I do
if I thought I had turned into
the parents
in that story? so poor
they had to send the children out
into the woods of a wicked witch? And what did
those people do when the children had gone?
Lie down and die?

Like so many stories, this one
has never made sense to me,
if it's really about poverty; so we read it for
the wicked stepmother, insisting it was she who
sent the children away. And we focus on the other
wicked woman in it, the woods-witch with her alluring
     sugar house,
and of course on Gretel, who's smarter than Hansel,
able to outwit the cannibal, and what about Heather who
tells this story because the boy she loves wants to be

her brother, while she is
willing to rescue him, like Gretel,
even though she'd like
to eat him up, she thinks he's so sweet
and tasty.
She's, in a way, just like the old
woods-woman, though she knows
she's no witch, just a lover who's never been chosen by
the boy she loves.
The daddy is the victim, and Hansel
is the one being
fattened for the oven, and all the women
want to be
loved; when they're not,
they look for sugar.

I am not sure this is a story
we ought to listen to,
we American women who are all overweight and
craving love
while eating sugar,
for there seems to be some sense
that we have to be witches,
though less greedy than the woods-woman.
We all think we are Gretel,
maybe because she's young,
not yet old enough to be a stepmother
or a cannibal.

Men are weak and helpless,
victims. That's the message, isn't it?
If all women are witches?

Good witches are young, beautiful.
Bad ones—you know,
   the opposite?

The Witch did not bleed where she was bitten, for she was so wicked that the blood in her had dried up many years before.

Frank Baum, *The Wizard of Oz*

THE NEW MOON, A SCAR

How can you see
something which isn't there?
  (The new moon is like a scar long
  healed.)
And how can you complain that you
have to die, when everyone has to? What's
the secret
of accepting this?

  She serves me a cup of coffee

and a white plate holding a thin wafer
of toast which I see as a sheet of paper on which
my father's written
his will: "Give my daughter
this officer's hat which used to
sit in her mother's closet."
Judith in Humboldt,
lightning bolt blouse a blaze
of Aztec fury, complaints
about the sex missing from her life,
but surely she must understand

the invisible by now,
the thing which is there but which
no one sees, or which is only a form
not yet illuminated.

I remember not eating my candy
when other children did, holding mine back till
I still had a piece of chocolate
when no one else had
anything but smeared fingers
or smudged faces.
"What a mean child you were," says the physician,
but I patiently explain to her
that I felt so out of control, my emotions were
so wild, my life so empty, my needs so great
when I was a little girl, that I learned early to find
what few moments of control I could exercise
in contrast to the actions of
other children.
    Now I say nothing

as my hair turns white
finally like moonlight and no one sees
the moon. I'm at last a full moon, with this shining head,
finally a mythic beauty glowing in reflected light,
but men and women alike see me as empty,
a new moon, nearly invisible, not a woman
any longer.

I walk across the bridge to meet
my lover. But I am almost invisible;
he doesn't even see me.
"Who is that woman with white hair?" asks someone
who should recognize me. I have turned into
my mother, my father's naval hat
with the gold anchor shining against the patent visor
is in my closet now, untouched.

Judith's gold blouse hangs in her closet. Old
women are witches better left unnoticed,
just like a scar,

just like the new moon.

"Oh, gracious," cried Dorothy. "Are you a real witch?"

"Yes, indeed," answered the little woman. "But I am a good
witch, and the people love me. I am not as powerful as the
Wicked Witch was who ruled here, or I should have set the
people free myself."

Frank Baum, *The Wizard of Oz*

HEALING GODDESSES

for Barbara Martin & Barbara Drake

Two Barbaras on Western shores heal me
with their lives. One Barbara
is in Oregon near
her late September grapes
  which this year

  will not ripen

for another month,
green as mossy stones right now, the rainy
summer having washed and washed
over them, a fast-moving brook
not clearing their surface, but giving
them a patina of verdigris; they will probably
make a thin, schoolgirlish
wine.

But each year is so different
she loves her life for its unpredictable
order, no chaos quite so beautiful
as the expected, where there is autumn
but it's not just one anticipated
color, one dependable
taste. Her sheep in the pasture are always
woolly and somewhat white, the vineyard
bears its fruit through the summer
and into fall, her garden snake
sheds its skin at predictable intervals,
but never looks quite the same,
the paper shell, like the bee hive on the
other side of the house, an emblem
of regular emptying, and the regular surprise
one remembers at the possibility
of finding it full again.

  The other

Barbara, with her white cockatoos,
her orchids and Persian rugs
in Northern California wine country reminds me
that surfaces can be perfect
with the discipline of thin china,
and the precision of surfing through the curl
of a wave.
  Like my Silver Surfer, she

moves through galaxies of Lalique
and polished wood, searching for complexity
which she then smooths into her ivory rug,
her table of pens and inks,
her hands like cowry shells
no texture without its contrasting
beauty: order in flux,
nuance, innuendo,
women with white teeth
and nautilus-chambered
secrets.

BOTTICELLI'S EDGES

for Judith Minty, a meditation on her poem, "Hawk"

Judith and I in the back seat: I
  behind the driver, her husband,
see myself in his rear-
view mirror.
My face, that is,
which I think of as sharp, hard edged,
like the talons of the hawk that she
found dead beneath her window and
cut off, removed along with the tail feathers,
to make a fetish,
knowing that to insure her human world
she was violating Dionysian order.
My face, though, is a thick mask of flesh,
wrinkling in this mirror and changing the crisp Diana,
Athene-huntress clear Slavic boned face into the visage of a
     hag.
No wisdom accompanies this

hag-face, only a melt-down to fat and bones
into the chaos of eternity. Judith sits beside me, earthy and
        empowered
by the stolen claws of her dead hawk. I still want
to see myself naked, with long golden hair, standing on the
scallop-shelled edge of the Pacific Ocean, my voice like a
diamond or an emerald falling inexplicably from my mouth.

Instead, I say "See this jacket,"
pointing to my well-tailored brown
Harris Tweed jacket,
worn over black turtleneck shirt and black jeans.
"I got it at a thrift store for $11."
I smile at Judith, wanting to please this bowsprit of garage-
        sailors,★
this Thrift-shopper par excellence. The smile
of Medea leaving Jason,
the gambler leaving the card table. "It fits you perfectly,"
        she says,
and I forget about
my crumbling face, perhaps
just an illusion in the car's mirror.
Her hawk eyes find me still sharp-edged,
reborn in somebody
else's Harris tweed jacket.

★*I owe the concept of "garage sailing" to Thomas McGrath's wonderful poem.*

"Which road leads to the Wicked Witch of the West?" asked Dorothy.

"There is no road," answered the Guardian of the Gates. "No one ever wishes to go that way....Keep to the West, where the sun sets, and you cannot fail to find her."

Frank Baum, *The Wizard of Oz*

YOUR SISTER IN JAIL

for Robert McDonald

She doesn't get it.
That when you start in
the middle of the dance
you still are expected to find
the rhythm, and to be able to go
with it, not against it. Who cares? she says, And
Fuck it, I'll dance to my own step,
and at the 7-Eleven she pulls a gun,
and makes them dance to her rhythm, they say yes,
don't hurt me, just take the money but there
isn't very much, we don't keep cash here,
it's a policy. She even
took your wallet, after you'd been good
to her, offered her shelter, a meal, some
sympathy and kindness, but then she
left with your wallet, your parents' car and your
father's gun that you didn't realize

127

she'd stolen the day before, and in spite of your brotherly
kindness she realized that
you too were dancing to a different rhythm
and once again she came on the floor
in the middle of the tune and furious at
always being late, never being in time, she said
Fuck it, fuck you, you're not really my brother anyway,
you're just like everybody else, telling me what to do,
I don't have to take it.

Now she's in jail, she writes to you, Please
write to me, this place is awful, it's just like
everyplace else, nobody cares what I think,
what I want, you always seemed to care,
why don't you write to me YOU'RE A FUCKING WRITER,
    WHY
DON'T YOU WRITE TO ME, here in jail where I am so
unhappy. And she still doesn't get it,
that when you start in
the middle of the dance,
you are/you always will be expected by everyone, even your
father, but especially your partner, the one you decide to
dance with, to find
the rhythm, and to be able to go
with it, not against it. Who cares? she says,
but you're her brother, and in spite of everything you do
care, it's just that there's no way to tell her that if
you followed her rhythm instead of the one that the band's
    already playing
you'd both be in jail, and what good would that do? She
wouldn't like that either, you tell yourself/why it is she can't
    seem to keep
time with anybody else?/must be genes, something missing
or something that shouldn't be there. You don't really buy
that, you know what it means to be different, but you've
never flaunted it, never ever felt the need to show
others that while you can do okay on the dance floor

you don't really like the music this band is usually playing.
This makes you know even more how little you could help
        her, your
sister, who's in jail right now and who doesn't really get it,
what you have to do to survive, and how survival isn't
a matter of necessarily liking the band, the tune, your dance
        partner,
or even dancing itself. You get it. Other people who are
        not in jail
get it/you do your best/fit in with the other dancers.

Then maybe, late in the evening,
when nobody cares any more, you talk to the band leader
and ask him to play something you really like, and
you get out on the dance floor, and really enjoy
yourself. When the band resumes, as it probably will,
the music you don't care much about, you don't
mind as much, going back to dancing the way everybody
        else
does, but you're secretly happy when someone comes up
to you the next day and says, "That was really a great dance
        you did
all by yourself out on the floor. Too bad your sister
        couldn't have
been here to see you dancing like that. Next time you
write to her tell her hello for me/you know I sympathize
        with
her frustrations, I just don't think robbing 7-Eleven stores
is a very good way of coping with problems. Hey,
        everybody's got
to find their own rhythm, that's what I say. I guess she still
        doesn't
get it/None of us really likes to, but we just
do it/we just get along, learn to cover up/dance the way
everybody else does, most of the time."

> "Maybe witches are just unhappy women with cats."

> *overheard in a mall*

WHITE CAT

Like the victory sign,
two fingers alert,
the ears of the white cat
are pointed at exact right angles
to her nose. Sitting in her
shop window, on Madison Avenue,
behind the glass of a handbag store window
she seems to
be approving, silently,
of this battle humans engage in,
fighting the city rain/the damp footprints
they track into her shop
are smudges on her landscape. She herself
unmuddied, dry and soft as the cotton balls
that rich women use to cleanse pastel faces, before
they soil them. This cat is tall, with her tail
curled perfectly around her feet/she could be
Egyptian, even the victory sign ears
a hieroglyphic, pointed to a sky which seldom
rains, one which encircles the earth as the body
of a beautiful woman whose toes touch one horizon
    endlessly.

The white cat of Madison Avenue

is sitting next to a handbag made of crocodile skin,
as if she can't distance herself too far from the Nile or its
Delta. Those ears keep reminding me of a victory sign,
two fingers raised and alert to everything,
the blue sky, the New York rain, the
melting women, gold beaten into ankle bracelets,
the heart weighed on a scale against a feather for truth.

DOGS

are a human
mistake.

Cats
are a way
to correct your
mistakes.

Fish
remind you that
brains are not
everything.

FAME

It can't mean that much.
There's no way to tell, when you dig up
a civilization, who had it
and who did not.

SWAN'S NECK

Consider the swan,
which is missing from my third pulse.*
Though a snake hisses in my veins,
and a frog seems to be in its mouth,
scarcely even the flap
of swan wings
sounds in my arteries. No swan in me,
except perhaps in my raucous voice
like a goose, mean, pecking
at strangers, and of course
there is my long white neck
still beautiful, but more like a snake,
a milky python,
thus more phallic, in imagery, in myth.

I thought for years
that he was a peacock;
and the only evidence showing I misunderstood
is *Who's Who*, and other biographical
sources which tell me of
his three marriages,
and then there's his love of Anna,
perhaps named for the hummingbird,
and his worship of Helen,
the Island beauty, surely enough connection with Leda
        there

*In Ayurvedic medicine, the physician learns to read the body's pulse as a
multiple. The three separate pulses are represented as the snake (vata), the frog
(pitta) and the swan (kapha).*

to make me understand
he's not a peacock, but a swan
among men?

That explains why, I suppose,
this man whom I have never seen other than in the
        company
of men—and who clearly has blanked me out of his mind,
even though my name is next to his, in every

reference work—why he treated me with such contempt.
I suppose he mirrors my pulse,
does not see my graceful swan neck at all.
Only sees me as Medusa,
snakes hissing out of my aging head,
as well as in my pulse.
So why am I hurt, offended?

Why am I worrying other than because he treated me
as if I were not a swan or even a snake,
but a piece of lint,
something to be brushed off his
coat?
I expected at least an angry
set-to, as if he, the swanny bird, had to fight for territory
with a ship or a serpent
or with something sea bound
that had a greater
measure than just a plain woman?
After all, we were just two vain creatures together.

This head on its long, insinuating neck, is a
question mark. It asks and
does not stop asking
why a swan is eyed as so much more
desirable than a snake. Or why a woman
should not have her share of white-swan love?

133

This made Dorothy so very angry that she picked up the bucket of water that stood near and dashed it over the Witch, wetting her from head to foot.

Instantly the wicked woman gave a loud cry of fear, and then, as Dorothy looked at her in wonder the Witch began to shrink and fall away.

"See what you have done!" she screamed. "In a minute I shall melt away."

"I'm very sorry, indeed," said Dorothy, who was truly frightened to see the Witch actually melting away like brown sugar before her very eyes.

"Didn't you know water would be the end of me?" asked the Witch, in a wailing desperate voice.

"Of course, not," answered Dorothy. "How should I?"

"Well, in a few minutes I shall be all melted, and you will have the castle to yourself. I have been wicked in my day, but I never thought a little girl like you would ever be able to melt me and end my wicked deeds. Look out—here I go!"

Frank Baum, *The Wizard of Oz*

at his Indian-giving head
every week, trying to pound
him into shape,
but he wants love
not virtue.

Across the room
is Beauty
taking a nap; he
makes me wish
my lifetime wish that I could remain
silent when I disagree. He has
no hammer, and knows it.
But he has the nails, nine-inch spikes,
somewhere in his tool room,
and he's learned a lot
just watching me hammer.

The other shakes his head at me. "I never gave
you that"
he says/ Oh, Olson, Oh, Creeley
where are the eyes of *polis* ? Not in their heads,
or is my virtue not enough?
Wood butcher on his island built a boat
to show his father he'd finally learned his craft;
my hammer, Beauty's nails, Steel Man
silent as a piece of oak.

The Tin Woodman knew very well he had no heart, and therefore he took great care never to be cruel or unkind to anything.

"You people with hearts," he said, "have everything to guide you, and need never do wrong; but I have no heart, and so I must be very careful. When Oz gives me a heart of course I needn't mind so much."

Frank Baum, *The Wizard of Oz*

EYE-VOICE

"I hear it," he says,
but he doesn't hear it or he
wouldn't open his eyes so wide to
answer me. He's always too cocky or
on the verge of being
frightened to death, his eyes widening
like a frightened horse, the
tension in his nostrils, the eyes too big, too
filled with abusive language, hard experiences,
crazy arrogance at surviving
his father, the city,
now lifting bags of flour
to work in a bakery,
cheating on his girlfriend
and brow-beating us
with his desperate
ambitious voice, the unlettered voice

that nevertheless could
be cleaned up and turned into
something spare, golden as wheat,
fresh bread rising. He's no McGrath,
though also Midwestern; I hear someone who is
skidding, speeding, trying to
win a race; win, not place or show. "You don't hear it,"
I tell him. "You're trying to listen
with your eyes." I close my own
eyes in hopes he will mimic me,
but I sense that his eyes are widening even
more, he's fearful as a horse in a barn that's on fire,
so I open my eyes and change the subject.
"Tell me about working
in the bakery." He relaxes and says,
"Oh, I don't work there any more."

THE EMERALD BOOK

to make a book; in betting, to lay the odds

Webster's New Universal Unabridged Dictionary

THE EMERALD BOOK

First it was a ring,
its stone of green glass
like an empty wine bottle
and on her finger, the watercolors
shaping the brush in large teardrop shapes
of sable, splashing even with colored juice, like
raspberries, the stain of coffee cup rings
adding to the paper's authenticity.

In China
she would have failed
with her bound feet and sharp tongue
like a rooster's beak, like a fighting cock
she would have driven everyone away.
Writing in the book, she would record
the ingredients for soup, and never listen
to the telephone ringing, calling with messages
of cancer or floods. In Poland

she would have eloped with Chopin
gone to the desert of Las Vegas where
they would have gambled
  for music and

the chips would be orchids, growing on the green felt
of blackjack tables. She would have avoided
nothing, the pansies, the snapdragons, the chocolate torte,
and the violence wouldn't have blown in like sand.

You search her room and there isn't a trace
of the Emerald Book. But she has it,
you know she does. Sometimes you watch her
dealing cards and see the green glass-stoned ring
flashing on her marriage finger.
  It's all "a movie,"
  as some dead poet said,
  "at the end of the world."

ORCHIDS GROWING ON THE GREEN FELT

blackjack tables, my hands holding
two cards
which equal twelve, oh why is
this number of the harmonious
twelve-tone scale, the octave,
so powerful in civilization and totally undesirable
in blackjack?

I don't have twelve fingers,
but who knows why five evolved, instead of six,
on to each hand/

the wisteria rope
has little white loads
of crystal.

We don't enough appreciate
how good smelling, how fresh
life is
in the 20th century,
in America, at least, how the torture
of the past

142

for many of us
would have been the daily smells
of grease, and smoke, of dried blood, urine
or feces, clothes unwashed all winter, partly for warmth.
Such smells would make the smoky casinos of Las Vegas
        seem
bright and fresh
compared to living in a one-room
farmhouse in Kansas
in the 19th century.
Snow seems so
clean, but would it be a
better way to die?
Is this blackjack table like a snowy field,
frosty with loss, or a rain forest where
orchids dangle like beautiful face cards
next to an ace.

  I see my story

like a twelve, not the twelve dancing princesses,
but a twelve you are dealt
as your first two cards, played differently
   depending on what card

   the dealer's showing.

Deal me an orchid, a phalanopsis preferably,
one that will fly away, a green moth
large as a spinnaker
held in my hand like a giant card.

Broken wings.

IRELAND

I asked
the Kewpie-cheeked college boy
who went to Ireland last year what
it looked like. He mumbled.
But in his modesty, he often mumbles.
He works in a half-way house, full time,
has been an undergraduate for six years,
working his way through school, is
proud of this and thinks
earning money is important.
He hates trained psychiatrists
and social workers
who wear their jobs like rubber Halloween masks
on their faces, and treat patients as if
they are also stamped out of a mold labeled,
        "schizophrenic,"
or "delusional." He wants to be a writer,
and that's why he went
to Ireland, he said.
Rocks on the coast, and lots of coast,
the rest an expanse of green, seeming more expansive
because of the relative lack of promontory ground.

Those are my words, not his, translated
from his embarrassed soft voice.
I make him nervous, in my opinionated way, always
quarreling with his
reality. "Are there trees," I ask
so he tells me about the two forest preserves

so small in comparison to American woods or wilderness
that you can walk from one edge to the other
in a very short time. I wanted to ask him
why he thought he understood what schizophrenia was
or how to treat someone who had it
better than did the doctors he despised,
and why if he cared so much,
why he was willing to spend years in school
studying poetry but not to enroll in any
courses that would make him a
medical professional who might
replace
the bad doctors and social workers,
who might do more
than just
pass out medicines to people who,
in his view, were only different
because they
needed freedom—
  like Irish rebels, or locals drinking in pubs—
Irishmen unused to trees
overwhelmed with the immensity of the groves,
even though these very "forests"
looked small to American eyes.

Instead, I kept asking him
to tell me about Ireland
because he escaped there last year
and is now dreaming of graduate study there
in literature, of borrowing more money to
stay in school so that he can get out of Health Care work;
yet his poems
are all about how much he'd like
to help people
while in his life apparently,
all he dreams of
is escaping

from the very world that
they live in. I accuse him,
make him more embarrassed:
  So he's working to have his Ireland
  but will not
  help them
  have theirs? I say. What a bad
person I am.
How
can I think these things
from my own sheltered life? I, who don't
like doctors, social workers, or mental patients,
though I admire the independent Irish,
willing to trade poverty
for the right not to be polite.
How I would like to be noble
for all the young men and women
who pass through my office.
How I wish I could myself believe
that we are worthy or
even slightly admirable for fighting
our own battles,
gambling on something
as invisible as poetry to change
the world?

Gambling is now bigger than baseball, more powerful than a
platoon of Schwarzeneggers, Spielbergs, Madonnas and
Oprahs. More Americans went to casinos than to major
league ballparks in 1993. Ninety-two million visits! Legal
gambling revenues reached $30 billion, which is more than

the combined take for movies, books, recorded music and park and arcade attractions.

Gerri Hirshey, "Gambling Nation"

Dear Craig,

I've been looking forward to the opening of the new MGM Grand Hotel in Las Vegas for several reasons. While I am more drawn to Luxor, the pyramid created by the Circus Circus enterprises, the advance information about MGM Grand intrigued me because I heard that an Oz theme was going to be used. The casino was going to be The Emerald City, and the MGM Lion I supposed would be transformed into the Cowardly Lion of Frank Baum's tale. I also heard that there would be sixteen (!), yes sixteen movie theaters in the hotel. At the moment there are no movie theaters on the Strip, and as a movie goer, I always wonder why not. (Sic. As a gambler, I can't believe I just said that!) I find it amusing that the only art movie theater in Las Vegas is actually in one of the casinos that caters least to educated or fashionable people, The Gold Coast, a casino extremely popular with locals and one where, as Steelman can tell you, they offer the best Keno payoffs in town. It's one of the several casinos with bowling alleys in them, but if you wanted to see *Much Ado about Nothing*, that was the only place in town it was playing.

I used to love the old MGM Grand, located where Bally's is now. Before it burned down, it was a place

I went to play nickel progressive slot machines and sitting there for hours at a time, learned to love the sound of the banks of dollar machines nearby, rattling their thunderous clank of silver dollars—back when the dollars used in many of the machines were actual silver dollars. At that time, the MGM Grand had a very plush movie theater in its downstairs arcade. All the seats were lavish armchairs and couches, sumptuously upholstered, and many of them had tables in front of them for drinks and food. They used to play old movies there. I remember weeping my way through Hepburn and Tracy's *Sea of Grass*, a movie made in the forties which is still very relevant on the subject of plant ecology and what happens when you artificially transform a landscape from grassland to farm land. The tragedy of the land parallels the tragedy of the human relationship in the film. Later, that theater was transformed into the Catch A Rising Star Comedy Club, which made much more money than a movie theater ever could. Actually, the club is now in the new MGM Grand, and I have no idea what's become of the old movie theater. *C'est la vie.*

I had hopes that MGM's reincarnation farther south on the Strip really would be filled with movie theaters. Alas, it is not. In fact, there is nothing much at the new MGM Grand which lives up to its name. The Lion is ugly, and that is particularly apparent when it is compared with the regal and awe-inspiring Sphinx replica across the street at the Luxor. The Emerald City casino is tacky, tasteless and—the worst—unimaginative. Outside, it is a green mirror-glass building, beautifully designed, a proper structure for The Emerald City, but inside it looks like Elvis Presley's interior designer at Graceland had charge of the casinos, lobby, and most of the restaurants, aside from The Coyote Cafe. None of it seems like Hollywood or Oz. In all fairness, I must say that Luxor, that architecturally magnificent pyramid across the street, is pretty equally dismal as far as interior design is concerned as well (though I suspect the hotel rooms are nice). All the carvings and statuary built into the design of the building architecturally are splendid, but once the architect left and the interior designers took over, you got dark tacky restaurants, like the bar where we had our drinks, which looked sort of like a fifties Tiki bar. What was that bamboo and South Seas stuff doing in a pyramid? I suppose to be fair to the MGM Grand I should only say that what's wrong with it is that they didn't issue us any glasses to wear when we entered the Emerald City. Emerald City in the land of Oz was certainly implied to be observer created.

This should mean that I could control my feelings better. Why can't I see Michigan as beautiful? Unlike the desert of Nevada and the neon city of Las Vegas which I find infinitely beautiful whenever I see it, the landscape of Michigan requires that I search for harmony, elegance or excitement. And, of course, I seldom find it. Yet, I cannot get out of my mind one of the few beauties I regularly experience about East Lansing, namely that I never drive down the main street at night without feeling as if it is an Edward Hopper painting, and I feel as if I am transformed into it. Another example of art making life acceptable?

Yr Lady of Observer Created Reality,

Diane

"My people have worn green glasses on their eyes so long that most of them think it really is an Emerald City, and it certainly is a beautiful place, abounding in jewels and precious metals, and every good thing that is needed to make one happy."

The Wizard of Oz,
speaking one assumes somewhat ironically.

Frank Baum, *The Wizard of Oz*

SEEING THE WORLD THROUGH HOPPER'S GLASSES

No longer a revelation,
like actually seeing an image in a crystal ball:
  when I drive down
  a certain street

here in this town,
at night,
I am in a painting by Edward Hopper.
At times, it takes my breath away,
    the way a candle gutters and surprises you
    that there is wind in the room:
to realize I might be
momentarily
in more than one universe.

No longer the moth
with huge wings like a green sail
that covered the doorway
I knew I should not enter.
    • broken wings?—

No longer stones falling out
of my mouth
of fireflies in the backyard
like modestly priced diamond rings
for very young couples,
floating around reminding us
that we love the phenomena of light
whether it lasts or not.

No longer a sense
that I could change the world,
though that is mitigated somewhat
by the fact that I have discovered its
multiplicity. Like a tiger
which appears to be so soft it might
shelter you, the light
is transformed everyday,
tricking us into believing in its
monolithic
singularity.

"Besides you have white in your frock, and only witches and sorceresses wear white."

Frank Baum, The Wizard of Oz

WHITE LAS VEGAS

This snow is all the games I play in Las Vegas,
which even as I watch it
in my backyard is visibly changing its shape.
Wet sugar, rivulets of snow.

My whole life has been a search for certainty,
the peaceful progression of the expected, and yet having
created this modicum, I long for a world which is all risk,
all defiance of the odds, all the pursuits of 98% loss to
        convince
myself there is always 2% win. I
live here in Michigan for its certainty,
while dreaming of the West,
while thinking of green felt tables, stacks of black chips,
the ringing of slot machines whose heavy metal sounds
        completely
hold me.

My friend's hands were gloved in snow when he played
blackjack once and lost two thousand dollars in five
        minutes.
But what's a hand, if not to be played? Las Vegas is radiant
        white

like new snow, like the good knight, gets the opening
    move
as in chess, reminds us of change, chaos, or complexity:
those the norm. And that's the miracle of the backyard,
created to revere seasons, where change is return,
return to certainty,
to the seeds which stay silent as part of the cycle
then deal green hands to me,
    summer basil,
    spring lilies of the valley or crocus,
    the second roses of autumn,
    the green of the juniper, or fir, or spruce
    no matter the season,
like the felt on the blackjack table
growing there all year, waiting for my visit
whether my hands are gloved in snowy age
or tan and bare
as the legs of a California girl.

"Well," he said with a sigh, "I'm not much of a magician, as
I said; but if you will come to me tomorrow morning I will
stuff your head with brains. I cannot tell you how to use
them, however; you must find that out for yourself."

"Oh, thank you—thank you!" cried the Scarecrow. "I'll find
a way to use them, never fear!"

Frank Baum, *The Wizard of Oz*

MARY'S DINER

Walk through the casino where the slot machine
bells ring your waist, a belt of sound
drawing you tightly into cherries, liberty bells, plums
on your way to breakfast. Tighten that belt,
stand in line, resisting the flash of lighted numbers,
the clank of coins. No jackpot could equal the bargain
      breakfast
at Mary's Diner, which must
be ordered before 9 a.m.

Sit at the counter where waitresses
like paper dolls from the forties
can be seen, never idle, making the toast,
refreshing the coffee, balancing plates and cups even
on their arms. Las Vegas business men
eat here, as well as tourists, gamblers
like ourselves, and old timers, retirees,
lots of smokers; this is Sam's Town,
away from the Strip or Glitter Gulch,
reputed to be the casino where the locals go.
A bowling alley, Keno paid at a higher rate.
Eggs, bacon, toast and coffee for
ninety-nine cents. Steelman and I pay
two-o-four, with the tax.
We leave a tip for the same amount, less
the o-four in case she thinks we mean it critically.

This is our Hollywood, the world we
fantasize, smoky and carpeted,

hands dirty from playing the nickel slots.
Each day a new day,
we begin with the sure thing,
the ninety-nine cent breakfast at Mary's Diner:
100% chance of winning.

Dear Craig,

I don't know if I can ever explain to non-gamblers the beauty I see in Las Vegas or why gambling attracts me as much as art, serious books, music or film. I also have no idea whether or not aging has anything to do with this; certainly I was not interested in gambling when I was young.

I do know that I am intrigued by the image of democracy that I see in gambling, where everyone has an equal chance to win and only a mysterious thing called "luck" seems to take away that equality. I continue to try to explain to everyone that I am calmed and reassured by gambling, being someone who seldom wins. I need to convince myself that in my life I haven't failed because I was stupid or because I was a bad person; I have failed because I played the game and lost.

Thus, unlike most people, I gamble as much to have the experience of losing—though I certainly don't like losing—as to have the pleasure of winning. When I lose, I feel as if my life wasn't all some large, terrible set of mistakes that I made. That what happened to me was simply the luck of the draw. Is this a way of renouncing responsibility?

More, I think, a means of forgiving myself, for I am full of blame. I burn and burn myself. I freeze myself with scorn. I am fire and ice with no sense of a temperate zone. If I criticize others, I criticize myself tenfold. I am always on fire or like an ice queen, freezing or searing myself with blame and judgment. To break even, I tell myself, is winning. And by the number of dollars I spend, I know how much it costs to win, since small wins have always been paid for with larger losses. I guess I gamble the way Catholics go to confession, to give myself some absolution, some relief from the terrible scorn I feel daily for myself and my life's failures. I continue to be grateful to you for our friendship, Craig. That I can tell you these things and that you are willing to understand.

Yr Lady of Flame and Fortune,

DW

AUTUMN

Eating lunch
at the roadside rest stop,
a circle of yellow coins,

falling.
Leaves so much lighter
than money.

THE SADNESS ON ROBERT'S FACE

It's always been there
when we talk about money.

I get excited.
With joy sometimes,
thinking of possibilities. Like flimsy
party dresses, which make a woman feel so beautiful,
and look so absurd, get torn and stained, lose
their butterfly-darting lilt, when worn home in the bright
      light
of the next day.

Or I get angry, thinking how much more the world owes
      me, the maid who
dresses the cream-shouldered woman who
fastens the clasp of that other woman's sapphires,
makes sure the satin bag contains a bill
for emergencies, who sits like Cinderella
when the house is empty, waits up
in case help is needed
after the party. My face, thinking of money, changes
as quickly as money changes hands.

But Robert's face, which should never
be photographed
when we talk about money,
is never excited and joyful,

and rarely is it angry, as it is when he drives the car;
other drivers invariably bring curses, wild shifting of gears,
sudden stops, and fast accelerations around offending
        vehicles often driven
by an old man
wearing a hat.
When we talk about money,
Robert's face
becomes the face I've seen on so many
pietàs. It becomes a face of grieving for the
lost child, the human one which for some moments always
transcends the knowing of that child's transformation,
his resurrection, his translation through
death.

Robert's face. I hate to say it. Ennobled
by suffering, the suffering I cause him
because I cannot ever learn
not to waste our money, not to misuse it.
He should be angry. I am not saving mankind. I am
not giving up what I have, for a greater good. I am not
investing in a better life or a better world, or even
buying something precious and worth sacrifice. He should
        be
more angry at me than the bad drivers on the road, but
he is the infinitely compassionate face of Madonna love
when he looks at me,
as we talk of money. I would like to deserve
this compassion. His sacrifice.
I would like to be the radiant.
I would like to be able to offer my failures
and with them save the world.

Instead, I see his face
growing stronger and wiser
and, like Demeter's,
she, who can never stop mourning

158

the loss of Persephone, even with the knowledge that
the beloved returns to the earth at least part of the year.

I long for California, where there is no winter, no
grieving mother, no necessity for forgiving or loss. But it
is part of my extravagant nature, part of my failure
to always believe in a world without winter,
or grieving. Without sorrow, or loss,
or waste. Robert's face
is the great face of all the myths of our culture. I should be
      the photographer
to capture this. Instead, I am only the dark shadow of the
Kore,
who must disappear, who is finally lost
in the crumbled
underground
of Robert's grieving face
when we talk about money.

...money was the narrow portal that framed his world and
through which he measured all its teeming phenomena and
events and inhabitants. A measure exact, reliable, and utterly
unclouded by lofty sentiment.

Tom Kakonis, *Shadow Counter*

EXAMINING MONEY

The little Darwin boy
with hair like a shiny penny
sits at a table
in the back of his grandfather's bank,
voyaging his fingers,
blunt nosed and sensitive, feeling each piece
of silver, moving like little caterpillars
sensing which direction to go, from flawed surfaces
to perfect ridges, his eyes
flicking like antennae over the coins for
the dates which are most collectable,
for numerals or initials
that might give a coin the uniqueness
of a new species.

Grandfather-president of this small town bank
approvingly nods, each afternoon
after school,
as the little boy comes into his vault,
as if he is boarding
the Beagle, ready to document everything
from fireflies to turtles if they are
recorded on metal currency.
He searches for coins he might
use in his
collection,
learning to savor silver
as his after-school snack, rather than a Frosty
or a Baby Ruth.

By the time
you started collecting, Craig,
there was very little silver
left in circulation.
At your grandfather's bank
the tellers
told
you
that you'd never find any silver; they had
sorted
all the money
that was in the vault.
  "They had holders,
  they showed them to me
  and they could look at the sides
  of all the coins before wrapping them
      • picked out the silver that way.
  I never found a piece of silver from the side.
  I always
  recognized it (the four pieces I found)
  by the metal
  from an obverse or reverse angle.
  It really
  used to catch the eye.

  I'd handled
  a lot of silver/I could
  probably pick out
  a piece of silver from ten feet/change
  on the dresser or
  something."

It is my image of you, Craig,
as the little boy, stubborn and sure
he could find things
the grown-ups could not, coming to Little Falls
to visit his grandparents,

insisting on the trips to the vault
that the tellers would say
were a waste of time.

You brought index cards
listing the dates of the coins you didn't have
in your books:
Lincoln pennies, 2 books,
Jefferson nickels, 2 books,
three Washington quarter books. Most of the silver
you had in your collection
was given to you,
as part of a collection started for you by your
mother's mother,
to be given to you
   "when I was a man, you know, mature—
   about 9 or 10 years old.
   I have a large silver collection—
   including every silver Roosevelt dime ever made,
   a book of Mercury dimes,
   many books of Washington quarters,
   Kennedy halves,
   Franklin halves,
   Liberty dimes. A few
   Liberty silver dollars."
Craig, little boy counting money. All that silver in your life!
But no silver spoon in your mouth, I think.
   "So, I'd have these cards:

Pennies, Book I

1911—S
1914—D
1923
etc.
Same for all the coins.
No one was really

collecting those pennies
at that time,
or those nickels; so I could
fill in many holes.
I didn't realize
as a kid
what value meant—
and that they were no longer making
Wheatear pennies—
that therefore they'd someday
be valuable.

Collecting must not be that fun
these days: all dimes, quarters and halves
from 1964 and back
are not in circulation.
There's not even much hope in collecting pennies
now.

I had some interest in buying coins,
but my father wouldn't go for that—
spending money to buy money.
I did look through quarters and dimes in my
grandfather's bank though,
figuring tellers might miss."

Craig, come visit me in Las Vegas.
We'll both dream of the Silver Surfer, not going
from galaxy to galaxy, but tumbling
from the machines, skidding
on silver nickels, Wheatear pennies,
Liberty dimes.

"The only time you get silver in circulation now
is when a kid breaks into a house,
steals a coin collection and then
spends it all on candy.

But there are
still some silver Jefferson nickels
in circulation,
mostly because many people don't know
they made silver nickels between 1941
and 1945; they needed
nickel/ for shells
and silver was, relatively,
unprecious
as war material.
Also,
Lincoln pennies of 1945 and 46;
you can notice that they are
sort of a yellow brown/we were
out of mining copper,
so to make pennies those years
our mint melted down
shells,
and you know
in 1943
we had no copper.
Made steel pennies,
those fine,
more silver than actual silver-
looking coins."

Let me tell you, Craig, why
men and women are different,
why
we like to see
men
as little boys but we see
little girls
as little women;
we see the lace and ruffle
over the downy skin and round knees
as erotic glimpses of the future

Madame Bovary,
the pouting sadness of a woman
to whom you make love.

It's that men are already so far beyond love
or softness. We need to see them
as little boys,
even in the realm of money,
counting silver,
with short chubby bodies,
wet hair,
and the serious look of concentration
before it becomes
a killer.
So,
I like to think of you, Craig,
at the age
when your love for money
was unusual and
touching, kindly even,
not manly, beyond what money is
to adults,
when coins are still beautiful,
like an orchid; when you can love them,
not what they buy. It's that little boy I like to think of,
Craig, your fingers like caterpillars, fuzzily touching
beautiful coins, inching over your
grandfather's coins in hopes
of finding something rare,
the shadow of your potential
Luna Moth wings
hovering over
the secrets of the past
with Darwin-like curiosity.

No, if he believed in anything at all it was the elegant symmetry of numbers, their cold austerity, stable precision. And against that kind of bare-bones beauty, all the words and signs and symbols were merely a stained blotch. Rise by the numbers, sink by them—either consequence was scrupulously grounded in a dispassionate equity. Which is more than could be said for most of life.

Tom Kakonis, Shadow Counter

ANNA'S HUMMINGBIRD

To you who loved the mysterious reference to "Anna"
they are all like numbers.
Small tokens or representations
of large facts or ideas.
A banker's grandson can find numbers
sexy, sensuous.
What you see when their long
beaks point into the feeder
or the trumpet shape of an orange flower,
or skim at the dried persimmons on
your balcony is
condensation.
So much female information
formulated into
humming
wings.

Quantum Theory #4: Heisenberg represented it as a matrix, Schrödinger as a wave; Feynman represents quantumstuff as a sum of possibilities. Classically the more ways an event can happen, the more probable its occurrence. In quantum theory, possibilities have a wavelike nature that allows them to cancel, so increasing the number of quantum possibilities does not always make an event more probable.

Nick Herbert, *Quantum Reality: Beyond the New Physics*

THE SUN BECOMES THE MOON

When the clouds cover the sun at noon,
that disk in the sky changes. And its light
is like moonlight, though dusty and
ragged, as if the moon rolled around on the desert floor
like a coyote and when it stood up,
sand shook out into the air,
dry as the seas
of the moon.

CHAMPAGNE LIGHT

Morning sunshine is like champagne
that you inhale. It sprays gently
against your crocus eyes, your purple finch cheek,

your anemone mouth, a fountain
into which you throw coins
wishing for a life which might never
end. The flute holding this light
gives you energy, you sip it,
no task seems impossible.

But as the glass empties and the day's light changes,
after the first glow of "anything's possible," your
body begins to feel heavy. You push yourself through
the afternoon. You walk or drive or talk to people,
you push your heavy self through light
which is more like a load of gravel being dumped,
and you running, scurrying like a sandpiper on the beach at
     sunset,
trying to get away from its crashing wave, its heavy
     tonnage.

In the evening, you lose the light entirely, but now the
     darkness
is like earth. You know you will eventually be covered
     with earth
and it will be comforting, or it could be, like the fluffy
     blankets
you pull up under your chin just before you go to sleep
     each night.
But for most of the evening, you continue to push it away,
push and push against it, as you have been pushing the
     heavy gravelly light of
afternoon off your shoulders.

Now it's packing down
against you, you never liked being in caves or enclosed,
comfort was space of the California deserts and ocean. You
     know
the pleasure of giving up, of falling asleep early under the
     blanket,

and then, throwing it off in the night, waking up to
        champagne
light, strawberries for breakfast; it's not just that the light
is beautiful, it's that you are light, unweighted, not even
        thinking
about the champagne hangover, the heaviness of limb
and how on some days you feel as if you have lost ground
        even
before it has covered you.
The champagne is finished. Now there's only night
or heavy day. And you might be made of moon rocks
instead of moonlight.

EMERALD LIGHT

Oz, left to himself, smiled to think of his success in giving the Scarecrow and the Tin Woodman and the Lion exactly what they thought they wanted. "How can I help being a humbug," he said, "when all these people make me do things that everybody knows can't be done? It was easy to make the Scarecrow and the Lion and the Woodman happy, because they imagined they could do anything. But it will take more imagination to carry Dorothy back to Kansas, and I'm sure I don't know how it can be done."

Frank Baum, *The Wizard of Oz*

LUXOR

On the points of fire
I burn my tongue, my fingers
spread around flames that turn into
butterflies. Yellow
finches at
the feeder
early summer, the spiderwort
buds still tight green balls
not revealing the indigo self,
iris, iridescent blue fire

the blue veins under my old skin.
Late in the history of physics
do we learn that blue is hotter than red,
my hands red from scrubbing,
my starry eyes
like candles on the table

dinner alone
I still eat with candles
I can't pass through this door
without burning myself.

CRAIG'S CALIFORNIA FIRE

The canyons where your bad luck comes from, Craig,
  like hummingbirds diving into a vat of red sugar water
  and emerging as candy, slick greens and reds,
  to snap and break on the glassy floor
are on fire.
I am asleep in the midwest
and there is a fire burning under my pillow
as I sleep.
  Like a hummingbird
  impossibly caged in a golden nest
  the fire flickers under the thick linen-covered feather
    pillow.
That fire is under my pillow every night,
but the bed remains cool.
My bad luck comes
from those same canyons, which
  like tunnels of fire
  led to every California house I ever occupied.
Where did I see the same reds of the ruby-throat?
  In my salty Navy dad with his St. Nick-red face?
  My ocean was not green enough to put out the fire;
then where did I ever find greens, like the ones
burnished against her ruby throat?
Surely not when I slept near the Laguna Canyon?
Or walked to Divers Cove?

When you walk in the wilderness
looking for rare hummingbirds and the flowers that
attract them, do you see someone watching?

Like a firebug, an arsonist,
  an unfortunate match? If you do,
it's your bad luck following you.
I cannot dream it away,
though I try, wanting to help you. I've
moved two thousand miles, but those canyons
lead right to my Midwestern backyard,
  tunnels to the fire under my pillow,
    fueling it with the long-range Santa Ana winds
    that blew around my Orange County past.

"There is only one thing in the world I am afraid of."

"What is that?" asked Dorothy. "The Munchkin farmer who
made you?"

"No," answered the Scarecrow. "It's a lighted match."

Frank Baum, *The Wizard of Oz*

ICE WALKING

When the candles are burning on the dining room table
like a cage full of canaries, and I am pouring a glass
of wine, my hand is steady but nevertheless
a few drops fall below the stem
of the glass on

to the scrubbed wooden
table. Apples piled up in a wooden bowl

reflect the light from the candles
like children's bedtime stories, and the little spill of wine
also shimmers. I am walking through the world
—no, gliding, or skating, but it's like flying, as if I would
          never
fall, it's not a dream, it's not liquid but the light which turns
          to ice;
it's my fear of dying, of falling, of breaking, of losing
everything. Yet ice has always seemed to be the way

others perceive me, with my hands of ice, and my eyes of
          ice,
and yes the Snow Queen lack of feeling I seem to display,

though the sliver of ice has always been, if anywhere,
in my eyes, not in those of some beautiful boy.
In my story, I am the Ice Queen, but the sliver of ice
is in my own eyes, and I see every boy as beautiful, every
handsome man as someone whom I would follow blindly.

This is all the ice walking I can do now,
balancing those drops of wine, like blood,
spilled under the glasses' needle stems,
the candles bubbling their waxy prisms
like fat yellow canaries
that fly away once they are mistakenly
uncaged.

WINTER SUNSHINE

Hard glint of reason
that follows the blowing filmy air—
yesterday's dark, receiving today's fluff.

On the other side of the
continent, Craig of Altadena is watching
his tank of Boesmani rainbows,
  of red-wag dwarfs,
   a continuing file of species
flirt through his room, selected for their colors, or because
     he
has never had one before. This is youth
arranging a life. In the midst

of this Michigan snow, I wait for whatever simple
birds will come to the feeder, and often watch it empty
of any species at all. You'd think I'd know for sure
each kind of sparrow that visits, instead of just the English
    or house
sparrows, which are really finches, and of course
the actual purple finches
with their recognizable color.

My life seems so dull that the world reflects it,
and there are days when even the worlds of Jane Austen or
    Anthony
Trollope or Margaret Drabble don't seem to be as
    interesting
as a road in the West might seem,

177

rippling out, stretching past fruit orchards, mountains,
sometimes the ocean, often long flanks of field or brown
        hills.
I know so may people who are never bored with
their lives that I have always felt as if
I were beneath contempt
for feeling as I do. This is no confession; it is middle-age
        itself
speaking, without urgency or pain or even
minor self pity or grief.
Myself, I have escaped from so
many of life's scourges
that I wonder if boredom isn't my reward,
sometimes, indicating
that its alternative would have been to die of AIDS
or to have been beaten
to death, or to have a son or daughter
who is a junkie or rapist.

Judith says to me, "You always have
someone faithful in your life, some man who is handsome
and smart, interesting. Like the son you never had."
I acknowledge this with gratitude.
Oh, it was so snowy yesterday, and I so tired,
and today the sun is like a very sharp kitchen knife
about to slip, fly with force into one of my eyes.
Your fish must be beautiful to you, Craig,
because you have such perfect control of them,
coordinating their colors,
manipulating their number, overseeing their
excellent health. The only control I know
is avoidance, the foot
hovering over the brake when I drive,
but very light on the accelerator too,
especially when there is so much ice on the road.

The King of Spain was the most I ever longed for,

and I never felt there were
a lot of fish in the sea. Imagine:
I didn't know what purple finches were
the first time I saw them!
Imagine not knowing so many things?

And failures. This light should slice away the failures,
it is so sharp that even a hummingbird wing
could make a shadow.

MYSTÈRE

Silence is a form of order
as when you enter a room in the morning
   when you've slept a whole night and everyone else is
   still sleeping,
      no matter whether that room is tidy
      or whether it displays a sink full
      of dirty dishes and a table
      with cigarette-filled ashtrays and
      smudged glasses,
         a bowl of stale biscuits
the quiet itself having rested like a blanket in that room
for some house, gives order
to the disarray.
Yes, you can clean it up and make physical
order, and in fact you do so because it is necessary
for as the day progresses there is
no silence,
no natural order,
and thus one must impose it
by cleaning, arranging, making new
possibilities. I used to wonder

how people survived
in great poverty,
the chaos inherent in a world without
even soap or water or broom
or vacuum, to say nothing of cupboards
of food. But now I know one of the cosmic
secrets.

Silence: the orderer.
The less that is
more.
Red cardinal flashing its color at my feeder.
He's chaos, not order.

DAVID'S LETTER

Your life was like snow.
It was perfect and frosted, but this
beauty would all go away/melt. You
needed to fill your life, so you bought
a planter box and a pack of cucumber seeds.
They sprouted, but you didn't see the beauty in
those little crochet hook shapes, pale as shod feet,

and did the strangest thing,
or to me it seemed strange. You dug
them up and stuck them back in the planter-box earth,
upside-down.
What a delicate touch you must have, as I
imagine even my own small fingers with their light touch

might press too hard had I done it,
pinching off cilia or crushing fragile nubs. But you did this,
    you said

in anger, and thus I should think a bit roughly, and yet
they all re-sprouted, came up again
like perfect little shepherd's crooks
the next day. Were they infinite seeds, or was it
you?

David, what's in those hands? Will anything sprout
from your green fingers?
Were you born to be a surgeon
or a jeweler? You could have stopped
the seeds from growing,
yet you couldn't change their potential shape
or color.
I once saw meaning in everything;
still have not given up the metaphor. But your letter from
    Berkeley
reminded me that I was wrong. We don't have destinies
unless we wrest them away from somebody else,
unless we insist over and over on
what we want and never give up something invisible
for something tangible.

Science's biggest mystery is the nature of consciousness. It is
not that we possess bad or imperfect theories of human
awareness, we simply have no such theories at all. About all
we know about consciousness is that it has something to do
with the head, rather than the foot. That's not much but it
appears to be more than the ancient Egyptians knew: the
Egyptians threw away the brain before beginning their
elaborate embalming the procedures, judging it to be a mere
accessory.

Nick Herbert, *Quantum Reality: Beyond the New Physics*

CLOSET OAKS

There is a door which I have
never opened, and I have no reason to believe
it would ever lead to a place I'd want
to go. But the door itself pleases me. It is like
the oak trees at the end of my small backyard in
      Michigan,
which, in the summer, are like full closets, their contents
completely obscuring
what might be in back of the clothing.

The oak leaves allow me
to imagine that instead of a street full of wooden houses
and beyond that another street, and beyond that two
      thousand miles
of American landscape, finally one could see the Pacific
      Ocean. I look out at the
summer oaks but know I am looking towards the Pacific, a
      possible
view of the ocean. That door is the same way:
there's nothing
immediately on the other side of it
which interests me at all, but just
knowing the door is there and that walking through
it one could walk into a room where I could find you,
waiting for me as you never did
in my lifetime—that is the thought I hold
in these summer mornings of
August when the blue morning glories
have finally started to bloom,

and our neighbors' moon flowers, as big as the elegant "V"s
    of glass
beer is served in sometimes, are wide open,
white as I imagine your body without clothes.

It is only my neighbor's moon flowers I touch,
not the man I look for,
  out through the oak trees,
  towards the Pacific Ocean.
  The sailor, my Jason,
  maybe he once was my father,
  or brother,
  but now he is
the King of Spain,
the invisible man beyond the oak trees:
yes, he might be
on the other side
of the door.

THE MOTORCYCLIST IN THE WOODS

The big red radishes,
strong and spicy, like that standing man
who drives a chariot
and lives with his horses at Delphi,
listening to "Horse Songs"
every day.
(They steam out of the hillsides and cave.)
A martini, clear
as rain,
the crunchy radishes,
some Vermont cheese, crumbly and dry
with its own starry grain.

The mystery, in any age,
was never what the rider
had between his legs,
  (horsepower)

whether galloping or revving
the engine, but how he
lost it.

The Pythoness
did not whisper, "drive, …"/
he said she told him
not to leave the track.
Watching the driver disappear
behind me, paralyzed
from the waist down, I am
in front of the mirror.
On the glass, steam
replaces my image.
Not prophecy
or even mist.

Perhaps juniper,
radishes,
a crumb of cheese to refresh you?

FROM SHELLS TO RADISHES

From shells, I have turned to radishes, eggplants,
cantaloupe, indeed the whole market place is a new
adventure—every day brings its fresh discoveries.
                                    Edward Weston, 1927

A blot of ink on the immaculate sleeve, like blood
spreading from my pen/he says he has
a long reach and he seems to be
talking about wrestling,
but I return to this image I have/of the dead
pelican lying on the beach at Pt. Lobos.
He laughs/he is a labor lawyer, I think,
but it was the actor, Reggie,
who found the ink spreading over his
immaculate cuffs while I wondered,
first 20 years later, then 30 years/
how the young poet could afford to collect
Beverly Pepper's heavy metal sculptures,
now displayed at the SF Museum of Art.

I'm on my way to the city
of neon sculpture,
where the Flamingo Hotel
reminds me of my own birth/what
does it mean to
control the images
in your life?

The camera's eye/ nonsense

all eyes are cameras
"North Dakota is everywhere"
says Tom McGrath, but
is it there in the light
or the flaxen purity of your words, Tom?

Touching with the eye:

museums are the brothels for those of us who are
afraid to touch. Here
there is no difference between a shell
a dead pelican, or a cabbage leaf. Nor a
woman's breasts. Why do I then need/
this glass of wine,

this cup of espresso?

"Emotion recollected in tranquillity"
"Each day brings its fresh discoveries"
Why can't I get his sleeve out of my mind? The blot
of ink spreading like flamingo wings,
or were they pelican wings? over
our only encounter in
twenty years?

"I am Oz, the Great and Terrible. Why do you seek me?"

They looked again in every part of the room, and then,
seeing no one, Dorothy asked, "Where are you?"

"I am everywhere," answered the Voice, "but to the eyes of

common mortals I am invisible. I will now seat myself upon
my throne, that you may converse with me."

Frank Baum, The Wizard of Oz

SOUND TRACK

Is there ever enough music to make the words sound
    interesting?

It was endless movie sound tracks—
Rachmaninoff's red wallpapered concerti,
swirling cloaks of Chopin,
"full moon and empty arms," which flooded
my moonlit childhood imagination,
offered images of women in ruffled black gowns
sitting at the keyboard of black and white movies,
so different
from the ugly images of femaleness
offered by my mother,
with her poverty-teeth bad breath,
her bandaged-flat breasts,
squashed in a lower class world that couldn't afford
uplifting undergarments,
her misshapen feet which had been squeezed into
cheap ill-fitting dance shoes.

Vanity and Poverty are a
violent marriage, Husband Poverty beating at,
decaying,
the Vain Wife's body.

Even her music was only played by ear,
a good ear with no models to imitate but rude country
music. How I learned that the greatest gift
would be silence, that the greatest beauty
came from good health and a few expensive
Katharine Hepburn/Grace Kelly clothes.
I was my mother's daughter:

everything that she was not.
And it was her choice of movies—Gene Kelly dancing,
Bing Crosby singing—that bent
my own sound track
away from flannel and tap-dance comfort.

So now I look for words which could
possibly offer something different, transcend the scores
which played through every failure
of my female life.
It is the purity of Vivaldi,
of Mozart, of Bach
I long for now.
Where the embrace is flowers, not humans,
cathedrals, not domestic buildings.
The spirit of life,
where love is ethereal
not physical, and death is not a surprise, but a composition
suitable
for my kind of movie's possibly silent
sound track.

Quantum theory works like a charm: it correctly predicts all
the quantum facts we can measure plus plenty that we can't
(such as the temperature of the sun's interior) or do not care

to (the electron's "piano attribute," for instance). This theory
has passed every test human ingenuity can devise, down to
the last decimal point. However, like a magician who has
inherited a wonderful magic wand that works every time
without his knowing why, the physicist is at a loss to explain
quantum theory's marvelous success.

Nick Herbert, *Quantum Reality: Beyond the New Physics*

BROKEN ICE

You think about the raped girl
and the broken fingers,
you think about losing
everything and then you
think about ice.

Ocean that was ice
no clove comfort,
no Danae chests bound with metal
bands, no linen wrappings,
no wedding rice.

How the glacier was a smooth tray
holding bones and teeth and gravel,
how the piano music could not
have sounded where you heard it
but it did.

Ocean breaks on
the rocks/the sound of emerald

ice in a glass, piano music
now tell me your (broken) story. I promise
I will believe you.

STORIES ABOUT MY LIFE

*One of John Cage's mushroom identification
stories, told as part of his lecture "Indeterminacy:
New Aspect of Form in Instrumental and
Electronic Music," on a Folkways recording that I
heard in 1959, is sort of a shaggy dog ("Shaggy
Mane"?) story. It's about an expert mis-
identifying a fungus, so that a poisonous one is
labeled as something edible. In response to the
query about how he could make such a mistake,
the expert replied, "Well, I specialize in the jelly
fungi; I just give the fleshy fungi a whirl." I have
always loved that statement, "I only give the
fleshy fungi a whirl."*

for John Cage

So wet this week, that if I had
a north side, it would
be turning
green, but the fleshy fungi
should flourish, emerge
just ready for omelets and the sauté pan.

Judith romanced
the mushroom man
chanterelle-basketed, chardonnay heady,
in Northern California. What a kind woman she is,
in her quiet voice saying, but slowly, "Diane, don't move,

190

on the tree trunk in front of you,
a little snake/I know you are frightened
of them." and I looking up the girth of the giant redwood
to see a slender foot-rule length with head alert
blending perfectly into the ruddy bark.
I'd been looking at the ground, especially at the base
of these trees, for mushrooms. She led
me away from my fear. I've loved the ocean beaches
of my Pacific, as they are empty of snakes, or so I've always
        thought.
Another day with Judith, this time in Michigan
on the edge of the Lake in North Muskegon,
sitting near a jetty, on the sand
with beach grass and weeds, there it was again,
narrow and short as a foot-long tape measure, its head also
        tilted
like a musical note, almost racing, a snake
where I thought there could be none.

How removed from earth I've always been,
but not without appreciation for what it yields.
No one knows about my own specialty
which is not really human. Like that other expert,
"I only give the fleshy fungi a whirl."

"It must be inconvenient to be made of flesh," said the
Scarecrow thoughtfully, "for you must sleep and eat and
drink. However, you have brains, and it is worth a lot of
bother to be able to think properly."

Frank Baum, *The Wizard of Oz*

WATCHING THE DRINKERS OF
GRAND MARNIER AT THE
PEANUT BARREL BAR IN EAST LANSING

Windexing the galaxy to
Andromeda swirls,
opening the asteroid belt,
traversing the Milky Way,
the Silver Surfer ignores the North Shore,
the pipelines in Australia,
he shimmers into East Lansing,
sparking to a stop,

  oh yes, he's looking for me,

the only one, like the King of Spain,
in love with my small self.
Like the Sphinx I am
sitting rigid with attention
in front of the winged boy
and his dark shadow.

Old filmy mysteries,

  Luxor, the woman
  with the crescent moon on her head,
flicker in the iridescent
compact disks whirling above the new juke box.
Amber, the syrup of ages,
is in the bottom of quiff-necked glasses.
Coffee with cream in

beer steins, half drunk,
unfinished business,
the beginning of a star-mission.

Like Cavafy, I understand looking and longing,
especially for beautiful boys, but unlike
the poet, I never imagine any
reciprocity. Instead, I hang out with
The Silver Surfer, The King of Spain,
The Bluemoon Cowboy, listen to the departing roar
of The Motorcycle Betrayer, know that I am safe
now in the homey arms of Steelman
whose scars match my own,
whose limitations match mine,
who promises never to leave me; and that's
the only promise
I ever wanted.

Quantum theory predicts the results of measurement with unsurpassed accuracy, but measurements are only part of the world. Most everywhere, most of the time, the world dwells in an unmeasured state. Anyone curious about reality will want to know what the world is like when it is not being measured. Quantum theory does not directly address this question.

Nick Herbert, *Quantum Reality: Beyond the New Physics*

SALUTING THE SUN

In Penn Park
we could always smell
eucalyptus leaves, like cough drops,
mingling their aroma into our hot dogs and potato salad.
The boys hated these picnics
where they had to be dressed neatly
with their hair combed and shoes polished
so the relatives wouldn't think
they might become gamblers or alcoholics.

Penn Park
was shady, even
on sunny days.
Our cousin Helen committed suicide after she
lost her husband to someone
in Australia;
I imagined koala bears
eating the narrow knife-leaves of these big scaling-barked
    trees.

The girls wore sun dresses,
my sister's and mine
covered with red
carnations.
Uncles wore hats,
aunts print dresses with heavy
slips. Big bosomed,
all of them, freshly powdered,
drinking hot coffee, even at a summer picnic.

We could not salute the sun,
breathe out, relax, fill up our lungs
with quantum space
or fresh *vata*.
This hemisphere was wrong
for us. Don't ask me why, imprisoned
in my chunky pale body,
my thoughts like eucalyptus leaves,
   my body like the heavy trunks of those
      Australian trees, the wrong species,
         mistakenly imported for making railroad ties
            that would connect all the Argonauts*
               gambling on finding the Golden Fleece
                  with the golden hills of California.

Dorothy lived in the midst of the great Kansas prairies, with Uncle Henry, who was a farmer, and Aunt Em, who was the farmer's wife.

Frank Baum, *The Wizard of Oz*

People who went West during the Gold Rush to seek their fortunes were called "argonauts."

THE BUTCHER'S APRON

When I was a child, we lived in the midst of orange groves on Russell Street in East Whittier, California, just up the road from the Nixon family grocery store, where I bought my popsicles from old Mr. and Mrs. Nixon, father and mother of the late president. When they expanded, adding a much bigger butcher's counter and a coffee shop, their son, Don Nixon, later featured in real estate scandals, became the butcher.

for Edward Allen

Red stains on the clean white bib,
the butcher's apron hanging like an abstract expressionist
     painting,
on the museum wall of my
childhood.

—the most we ever ordered—
a pound of hamburger
to be fried in the black iron skillet
till the edges formed an ugly crust
like a scab on a skinned knee/
The art of the grill
was not found in our manless house.

The beauty of the red on the butcher's
white canvas, which occasionally streaked like an etching
across the white butcher paper

in which he wrapped the chuck, never translated
to the food eaten: grey meats
like steel wool, canned vegetables
with the colors of hospital walls,
sliced white bread like old often-washed
sheets and pillowcases.

My shock one day in the school cafeteria
to see Carol Gregory
   whose mother sewed her
   dresses as elegant as those in
   Vogue magazine
unwrap a waxed paper packet of bright red
meat, in a puddle of something thin and dark/
to realize it was
Roast Beef,
the puddle
was beef blood! There in the Lowell School cafeteria
I saw my first still life painting, beautiful and
different food among the thermoses
of milk, the wax-wrapped peanut
butter or bologna sandwiches. Perhaps
I have added this detail
   next to Carol's rare roast beef slices,
   another piece of waxed paper on which
   was spread
      several spears of bright green
      asparagus.
Food eaten by kids whose parents were rich
or had been to college
was different,
was like a painting?

My first generation American mother grew up
in a house with a dirt floor, went to school
in a one-room schoolhouse. She drank German
coffee instead of milk

as a child. She lifted herself out
of North Dakota, became a bookkeeper
but never learned
about food, the telltale class
marking. In old age, she loves salty things like
Campbell's soups, frozen enchiladas in processed cheese
    sauce,
bacon white bread sandwiches and hates the nursing hospital

where they don't salt the food at all.

Plath imagined blood red tulips in white hospitals
as I think of Georgia O'Keeffe's poppies.
My mother who voted for Nixon and hates foreigners
dreams of those red and white cans
which might hold chicken noodle or tomato
soups. She's never heard of Andy Warhol who
mimicked such cans, just as a butcher I talked to in our
    Michigan
supermarket said that he had never eaten
shrimp, or knew what people did with oxtails. His apron
too had the same bright red stains, not yet faded into
rust. Crimson blood on canvas, the art
of childhood. Unhealed scars,
still capable of bleeding.

Quantum Reality #7: (Consciousness creates reality.) Among
observer-created realists, a small faction asserts that only an
apparatus endowed with consciousness (even as you and I) is
privileged to create reality. The one observer that counts is a
conscious observer.

Nick Herbert, *Quantum Reality: Beyond the New Physics*

HOT FLICKERS/MOVIE LIGHT

still thinking of images from Top Gun

The highway along the coast
with its little beach towns, where the sinks
were discolored with necklaces of alkaline water from rusty
      pipes,
and the papered walls of bungalows always smelled wet, or
      moldy,
turns into a film at sunset, when the lovers
walk like a flamingos on the beach
as they never did
in real life. The natural gas
wells pumping, across
the highway, the black stained
steely heads of the dippers
setting a rhythm no one would ever
dance to.

  Inside this frame,
she's riding a motorcycle along the highway,
behind the leather-jacketed pilot,
her head full of mathematical equations,
aviator glasses with amber lenses disguising her;
she could not be farther from him if she were on another
continent. But their bodies nested together
on wheels,
  as they ride the coast,
    or the desert highway into Las Vegas,
could be hot flickers to the eye

199

experienced at the Odeon, or some other
movie palace.
   Outside this frame,
she is Diane, the Californian,
the dull unnoticed daughter of Jeffers.
   Outside this frame: she is wearing glasses,
the class brain,
simultaneously stationary or
whizzing by.
   Inside this frame,
she is the princess
of orange groves, and he the rider
coming out of the surf.
The line on the highway draws them

into the distance.

STARLIGHT

Some of it
from a thousand years ago
still crisp, not even
slightly
crumbled.

MEDEA'S CHILDREN

Like Sappho's dawn
would they wear gold sandals?
If I were Dorothy,
I would give them the Silver Shoes,
or if I were Judy Garland,
I'd hand over the Ruby Tapdance Slippers in a minute
so they could go home, or find their Jason-fathers,
who'd give them kingdoms, not stepmothers who'd
send them into exile, But my closet
is filled with aerobic shoes
and Birkenstocks that disguise old
treadmill feet; I'm not Diana, lily foot on the sickle moon,
just her creator; or perhaps I'm
the Witch of the West,
old, having already offered my own
sparkling footwear
on an altar.

If it is up to me, they must go barefoot
into the wilderness,
or steal their own foot coverings
from the morning's radiance.

Dorothy stood up and found she was in her stocking feet. For the Silver Shoes had fallen off in their flight through the air, and were lost forever in the desert.

Frank Baum, The Wizard of Oz

Printed June 1995 in Santa Barbara & Ann
Arbor for the Black Sparrow Press by Mackintosh
Typography & Edwards Brothers, Inc.
Text set in Monotype Bembo by Words Worth.
Design by Barbara Martin.
This edition is published in paper wrappers;
there are 250 hardcover trade copies;
125 copies have been numbered & signed
by the poet; & 35 numbered copies with an
original holograph poem have been handbound
in boards by Earle Gray & are signed by the poet.

Photo: Robert Turney